THE SOUL HAPPY BOOK

Tracy Zboril, MSW
Cara Hewett, MA

SOUL HAPPY

Copyright © *2018 Soul Happy*

All rights reserved.

Published by *Soul Happy, 2018*

Winter Park, FL

Edited by Jenny Lee Corvo

PRAISE FOR SOUL HAPPY

"Very powerful... simply outstanding!" – *David, Gainesville, GA*

"Thank you for coming into my life. What a change you have shown me. You have turned my life around at the most critical time." – *Lauren P., Windermere, FL*

"This modality is effective and can be used again and again for refinement and evolving." - *F.A., Orlando, FL*

"I like the idea of reprogramming your brain and neuroplasticity in general. I've touched on this in my own reading, it seems so familiar to me. It kind of reminds me of the law of attraction. I know you can help a lot of people." - *Tara K., New Jersey*

"It's so weird, when I think about this memory, that had just overwhelmed me with emotions, it now seems like it's over there, over in the corner, like it's not important. That's so cool!" - *D.F., Ann Arbor, MA*

"Now when I think about those memories, they seem to have lost their charge," – *Kelly R., Winter Park, FL*

ABOUT THE AUTHORS

Tracy Zboril, M.S.W

Tracy has been in the field of psychotherapy since the 80s, practicing in various genres including grassroots in-home therapy, in-patient psychiatric hospitals, out-patient clinics, therapy within a public school system, and almost 20 years in private practice. In more recent years, her focus shifted to the mind-body-spirit connection and she started exploring and studying new modalities including integrative models, transpersonal psychology, human consciousness, hypnosis, along with new advances in neuroscience and the energetic field of quantum physics. As passion for this knowledge expanded, her desire to change her clinical focus resulted in a collaborative effort with her like-minded colleague, Cara Hewett, and the Soul Happy Technique was developed. This technique uniquely combines all these various fields of study.

Cara Hewett, M.A.

Cara has been in the field of psychology since the late 80s. Her experience includes in-patient psychiatric hospitals, mental health agencies, private psychotherapy practice, as well as teaching and counseling at the university level. She is trained in various therapeutic modalities including EMDR and hypnotherapy. Her understanding of behavior from a transpersonal perspective led to forming a mind, body, spirit center which offered classes and workshops in personal growth.

Her passion continues today with further emphasis involving theoretical approaches in the field of psychology, metaphysics, neuroscience, and the study of human consciousness.

The Soul Happy Technique developed with her colleague, Tracy Zboril, was researched and developed based on the latest discoveries in these fields of study.

About Soul Happy

The Soul Happy Technique combines therapeutic models rooted in neuroscience and energy theories behind quantum physics to offer an innovative and powerful method that helps people overcome disappointments, traumas, fears and past failures that often get in the way of true happiness. By tapping into the subconscious mind and reprogramming the negative feelings stored there, the technique helps alleviate anxious and insecure feelings we experience as part of our everyday lives. The Soul Happy Technique gives you the tools you need to become the best version of yourself before the negative memories and feelings you experienced throughout your life got in the way.

Find Out More: SoulHappy.com

TABLE OF CONTENTS

Tracy Zboril and Cara Hewett

PREFACE

The Soul Happy technique was born out of our frustration with the limitations of traditional psychotherapy. As seasoned therapists with over 40 years of combined experience, we consistently ran into the barriers of therapeutic models that were time-consuming, costly, and often unsustainable. It was not until we discovered the ease and effectiveness of hypnotherapy that we began to see the possibilities of working directly with the subconscious mind.

A synchronous meeting at a hair salon after a hypnotherapy conference led to a powerful partnership that became the foundation of the Soul Happy technique. We realized that we were both butting up against the same limitations in our psychotherapy practice, over and over again, and something had to change. For us, exclusively offering talk therapy was a way to keep our practices open but fell short of one huge factor - authentic, long-lasting, sustainable change for our clients.

Of course, we began our careers as therapists because we wanted to affect change and encourage healing in the wounded. Seeing the ineffectiveness of the techniques we'd been taught was discouraging. Looking back on our careers, we understood that it wasn't psychotherapy that was the problem, it was the approach.

It was at this point that the Soul Happy technique began to take shape. While our hypnotherapy training gave us the chance to work with the subconscious, which was proving to be effective, there still seemed to be something missing. We realized that we wanted to give people the opportunity to become deeply tuned in to their core self, where all their strengths exist in their purest form. We wanted to give people access to their superconscious, where permanent change and impact can really take place.

Our research and study took us into fields far beyond what we'd learned in our psychotherapy and hypnotherapy training, like quantum physics. Compiling the research and finding the common threads was no easy task, but the result was a technique, unlike anything we'd ever seen. We decided to meld many theories together to form a sequence that could address the mind and the higher self - the core of the self - our soul. We blended hypnotic induction, neurolinguistic programming, guided meditation, and what we call Subconscious Imprinting, which utilizes the senses, the language of the subconscious, to imprint future positivity.

After practicing the sequence with our clients and receiving incredible results, we decided to get the technique out to as many people as possible. We thought, "Why not provide this technique to masses of people and better yet, use it in the privacy of their own homes via the internet?" So, we began with writing this book. Our task in this book has been to accumulate a daunting amount of intellectual material and distill it down to a meaningful, tangible concept and put it into a viable therapeutic framework.

Our hope for this book is to demonstrate the long-lasting value of the Soul Happy technique. To do this, we have organized the book into two parts. Part I details the research behind each aspect of the method. Some of this research involves the fields of neuroscience and quantum physics. In these sections, we aim to deliver the information thoroughly, but accessibly. We want to demonstrate the cutting-edge research that influenced our technique without being overly technical or, frankly, boring. In Part II, we detail the four steps of the Soul Happy technique. While this book is not a substitute for practicing the method, we wanted to show exactly how we applied our research into actual practice.

We're enormously proud of the Soul Happy technique because it works. We've watched our clients' lives change in ways they never thought imaginable. Moving beyond addressing the symptoms of anxiety and depression that are a result of adverse experiences, our clients have been able to tap into the deepest parts of their mind – of their soul. We wish the same for you. Thank you for taking this journey with us.

Love,
Cara and Tracy

INTRODUCTION

Imagine a world where people live purposefully because they are attuned to the deepest core of themselves, one where people have confidence to manage stress at every level with grace and fortitude. Who doesn't want to live there? As therapists, it's our life's mission to make that world a reality by helping people become the healthiest version of themselves. Unfortunately, the prevailing system of psychotherapy that relies on psychiatric drugs and talk therapy wasn't furthering our mission. Something was missing, so after years of research and trial and error, we developed a way to make it happen - the Soul Happy technique.

If that sounds like new age BS to you, don't worry. This is not another self-help book telling you to stare in the mirror and say you're beautiful, loveable, and happy over and over again until you get it and therefore believe it. In fact, positive self-affirmations alone don't work, and after reading this book, you'll understand why. Instead, this book is an explanation of a technique that is based on science, experience, and research.

So, what should you expect from this book? First, it's important to understand that the Soul Happy technique is experiential. We can't expect you to read this book, follow the directions and then clear emotional blocks hidden in the subconscious mind. Instead, this book is a primer, or foundation, for the sequence.

We'll begin by detailing our research and experiences with our clients. We've laid out these concepts in language that's easy to understand. We're not going to give you a discourse in quantum physics. Instead, we'll keep things simple. We did all the heavy work and distilled it down for you to read and understand without needing any background in the science behind it.

We're going to tell you how your mind has been programmed since early childhood to react a certain way, and then we're going to tell you how memories are stored and processed. Then, we're going to show you how it's possible to change the way you think. You'll see how you can generate significant positive change in your personal lives, careers, athletic abilities, academic challenges, and more. You'll understand why you have blocks or hurdles that prevent you from producing beneficial thoughts.

The Oprah-Chopra Balance

When writing this book, we often wondered if it was possible to distill all this information in an easy-to-read format. We asked how we could write about these sometimes-complex theoretical concepts and put the data into plain English so that anyone could grasp what we're trying to say. We wanted to get our point across in a way that reached the right balance. It became apparent to us. We needed the Oprah-Chopra balance.

These two icons of personal development perfectly represent the combination of mass appeal and brilliant scientific understanding of human consciousness. By using this approach, we're not suggesting that our accomplishments are in line with theirs. Instead, we're using their names as role models and modern-day archetypes. We're pulling from both what they represent and how they've presented those concepts for the benefit of promoting human potential.

Like Oprah, we'd like this information to reach the masses. (Plus, we just love her.) Like Chopra, we bridge concepts of neuroscience with spirituality. In our view, all of humanity would not be able to comprehend these new mind-body concepts without the platform of Dr. Chopra's 30 plus years of groundbreaking work. While writing, we often checked in and asked ourselves if we're hitting the right Oprah-Chopra balance.

The Influences Behind Soul Happy

We want to take a moment to acknowledge the influences of the Soul Happy technique. To develop this technique, we had to understand and blend a myriad of philosophies, studies, and research findings that encompassed ancient teachings combined with the latest theories of intellectual modern-day thought leaders. We've spent considerable time researching and finding common threads that validate and complement each other to form this useful therapeutic technique. It's an alignment of a series of complicated, sometimes overlapping concepts.

All the modalities we are going to mention are fantastic at healing the mind, and we certainly recommend, if you are so inspired, to research these techniques and try them out for yourself. Such modalities include, hypnotherapy, Eye Movement Desensitization Reprocessing (EMDR), Emotional Freedom Therapy (EFT), Rapid Resolution Therapy (RRT) and NeuroLinguistic Programming (NLP).

Some of these therapy models were created by individuals outside of the field of psychotherapy, proving that healing the mind reaches far beyond simply an understanding of psychology and requires a deeper understanding of science and technology. For instance, EFT was developed in the 1990s by Gary Craig a Stanford trained engineer. And NLP founder, Richard Bandler, a mathematician, composer, and philosopher became interested in hypnosis after meeting hypnotherapist, Milton Erikson.

In our research, we were especially intrigued by Dr. Jon Connelly's Rapid Resolution Therapy. We both received training in RRT and have been inspired by the transformative nature of this technique, which incorporates the use of stories and metaphors for communicating with the subconscious. We owe Dr. Jon Connelly much gratitude.

Another predecessor to whom we are gratefully indebted is Richard Bandler. An important part of our technique is the process of clearing out the buildup of past negative memories. This clearing process utilizes some of the techniques originated by Richard Bandler's Neuro Linguistic Programming (NLP). Bandler's work enables a processing of memory in a way that is similar to dissociation. In other words, once a memory is processed differently, it can no longer carry the negative charge that it previously carried.

Bandler's work focuses on using slowed down brain waves states to access the subconscious mind, where memories are then scrambled so that they can be disconnected from the intensity of the original event. These mental exercises have been widely used since the 1970s and you'll see much of this influence in the coming chapters.

Another technique we believe is extremely powerful and was of great influence to us is the Emotional Freedom Technique (EFT), also known as tapping. EFT is a process that stimulates meridian points on the body's energy system. Meridian points have been noted for their curative potential since ancient times and provide the basis for acupuncture and other Eastern healing modalities.

We've also utilized the groundbreaking work of Dr. Joe Dispenza, the bestselling author of You Are the Placebo, and Breaking the Habit of Being Yourself, and his latest work, Becoming Supernatural. Dr. Dispenza has changed the way many professionals view the subconscious mind's ability to heal our bodies, and his discoveries have significantly influenced the development of our technique.

Dr. Deepak Chopra, who needs no introduction, has also greatly influenced the fields of neuroscience and quantum physics and has also been integral to the development of our approach to addressing the subconscious mind.

The work of Carl Jung, Joseph Campbell, and Dr. Clarissa Pinkola-Estes has also helped us understand the importance of story-telling and archetypal images, and how we conceptualize thought and learning through images and visualizations.

Transpersonal Psychology, one of the latest theoretical approaches to human development, has also inspired us. The techniques within this school of thought include the study of the mind-body connection as well as spirituality and consciousness. This new paradigm of viewing the individual as part of a collective is thankfully beginning to replace the old behavior-oriented model of psychology.

Finally, we have also embraced some concepts related to eastern philosophy, ancient universal laws, and the understanding of human consciousness. Elements of meditation, mindfulness, and Eastern philosophy are also included in a very significant portion of our technique which we call "expanded awareness," in which the goal is to get you in touch with your authentic self - who you are at your core where all your strengths exist at their purest form.

You'll likely see some of the inspiration sprinkled throughout the book, but we do want to recommend once more that you investigate these techniques alongside your study of Soul Happy. While not all of them are included in the Soul Happy technique itself, we have included many of the exercises in Part II of the book, so that you can use them in tandem.

Let's Get Started!

Now that you understand what to expect from this book let's dive right in. We're going to share some fascinating information with you about energy, neuroscience, psychology, and spirituality – everything that serves as the foundation for our technique. Then we'll guide you through the details of every step of the process.

By the end of this book, you're going to understand how you can shift the energy of your subconscious mind and affect genuine, radical, lasting change in your life. Anyone can make this change happen – even if you've never tried psychotherapy before, or you've tried every imaginable method and seen little to no results.

PART I:

The foundation of the Soul Happy technique

Tracy Zboril and Cara Hewett

CHAPTER 1: THE POWER OF SELF

Now more than ever, there is immense pressure to a be a high-functioning professional. We'd even argue that the pressure isn't just to function well, but to function at nearly impossible levels. Living in our current society often means struggling to balance the incredible expectations at every level of your life. More than likely, your days are full of trying to be a perfect employee, a perfect boss, a perfect spouse, a perfect parent and a perfect friend. If this sounds familiar, you're not alone. The rise of convenience and technology means everything is expected to work faster and better – including you.

But you're not a machine and whether it's easy to admit or not, perfection isn't possible. The smarter and more ambitious you are, the more likely you are to try and grab it all, and the more compassionate and empathetic you are, the more likely you are to try to be everything to everyone. Of course, social media hasn't helped in that department. It can often feel like we're living in constant comparison to other people's achievements.

This is the nature of the reality we live in today. The pressure is on. The expectations are enormous. And it feels like everyone is watching, waiting for you to succeed or fail. It's easy to intellectually know that this pressure isn't healthy, but we can't blame anyone for trying to meet these demands. Instead of trying to convince you to approach the expectations differently, we want to offer something different. We want to help you cope with the inevitable problems that come with aiming for perfection at every turn.

Like we said earlier, when you're smart and ambitious, it's difficult to aim for anything but perfection. If your natural drive is to put pressure on yourself to succeed, you're not going to easily back down. Instead, we actually suggest using that ambition and motivation as your greatest asset on your path to becoming the best possible version of yourself.

Because the reality is, you can change. You can heal. Depression, anxiety, or any other mental distress you might be facing as a result of all these pressures, they can be transformed. In later chapters, we'll discuss exactly how these transformations take place on the physical level inside your brain. In the meantime, we want you to feel empowered to make these changes because you have more contribution to those transformations than you might currently realize. But don't be mistaken, these changes won't happen overnight, and they won't happen without action and effort.

We Want Our Quick Fixes

With all these expectations and demands, it's not surprising that many of us suffer from anxiety, depression, and a host of other psychological and physical symptoms. This demand for everything to move faster and better means we also tend to expect fast and easy solutions – even to the problems caused by those expectations.

When you look at it that way, it seems a little silly doesn't it? We suffer because we expect urgency and perfection, but then we turn around and expect immediate and simple solutions for that suffering. We want someone to identify our issues, name them, and offer a solution. We want to know what's wrong and what we can do about it – the faster and easier those answers, the better. Again, we're not here to place judgement on those demands. Despite how silly it might seem to expect quick solutions, it also makes total sense in the world we live in. You're likely constantly inundated with those promises.

Resources for solving practically every problem are available instantly and at our fingertips. Need parenting advice? Follow five child experts and read their latest articles. Want the latest nutrition information? Follow healthy eating blogs. Advice on common childhood ailments? Follow a community board. Trending fashion? Instagram. Home décor? Pinterest. Travel ideas? Conde Nast website. Touch base with friends? Facebook. Immediate solutions seem to be everywhere – free and easily accessible to most of the world.

And the same is true even with our face-to-face needs. Not feeling toned? Schedule time with a trainer. Want to look more polished? Schedule a mani-pedi. Aching? Massage. Aging? Facial. Cramping pain? Acupuncturist. Feeling hormonal? Schedule an appointment with that nurse practitioner at the OB. Adult acne? Dermatologist. Mood swings? Stress? Anxiety? Schedule an appointment with your therapist.

But take a moment to look at those solutions. Do any of them offer permanent or long-lasting transformation? They might be easy, quick solutions, but do they have any sort of longevity? Of course, they don't. And you're probably aware of that on some level, but the sheer amount of convenient, temporary solutions is overwhelming, and let's face it, easy.

It only makes sense that we'd apply this same type of thinking to modern day therapy too. We've gotten feedback from so many and found that, sure enough, a lot of people do go to their therapist simply for quick directional advice or to vent and unload daily injustices. Leaving there, they feel a sense of release of negativity, and they can then head out to family and friends with a new, refreshed attitude. Just like the other quick-fixes we've mentioned, it's a great temporary solution, but approaching therapy with that expectation can't result in long-lasting change.

Feeling anger? Get diagnosed with adjustment disorder and go for EFT (Emotional Freedom Technique). Traumatic experience? Get diagnosed with an anxiety disorder (GAD) not otherwise specified (NOS) and go for RRT (Rapid Resolution Therapy) and Xanax. Scared of things? Get diagnosed with PTSD (Post-Traumatic Stress Disorder) or phobia disorder and the protocol is EMDR (Eye Movement Desensitization Reprocessing). General problematic behavior? Go to NLP (Neuro-Linguistic Programming). Addictions? Get diagnosed with Substance Abuse Disorder and go to a 12-step program. Hyperactive? Get diagnosed with Attention Deficit Disorder with Hyperactivity (ADHD) and get treated with biofeedback and stimulants. Depressed? Try CBT and (Cognitive Behavioral Therapy) and Prozac. Marital discord? Try on Dysfunctional Relationship Disorder and go for ECT (Effective Couples Therapy). Tics and jitters? Get diagnosed with OCD (Obsessive Compulsive Disorder) and get on some meds. Bummed out in the winter? Get diagnosed with Seasonal Affective Disorder (SAD) and get a sun lamp or plenty of antidepressants. Hyperactive? Are you a pain in the ass? Get diagnosed with Borderline Personality Disorder (BPD), but sorry; there's no treatment for that. Sexual Dysfunction? Psychoanalysis and Viagra. Okay, you get the picture.

We're exercising hyperbole to really drive the point home that therapy no longer carries the stigma it once did, and with this new category of relief-seekers using therapy for benign, general coping purposes, many more people are heading to the therapist's office than ever before. In addition to those seeking treatment for more deep-rooted issues and chemical imbalances, there is also now a significant segment seeking the support and connectivity that the ongoing therapeutic relationship provides.

We're Looking Outward When We Should be Looking Inward

Every treatment modality mentioned above has its merit and value. But after utilizing the above diagnoses and treatments for years, we can't help but notice that they all encourage people to look outward to specialists for quick answers and quick fixes.

Get a label; get a fix. Get another label; get another fix. This emphasis on instant answers to deep problems causes us to miss an important strategy – the ability to sit with an uncomfortable experience. Our society has trained us to look outward for the answers to anything that causes the slightest distress or discomfort.

There is a better way. Many of the most valued thought leaders of both modern and ancient cultures have stressed the importance of listening to the intuitive voice within. It turns out, all the answers we need to flourish are found inside each of us. While it's good, common sense to seek out information from experts, we ultimately must decide on our direction - own our healing.

The more capable we become at making our own decisions, plotting our course of action, and taking responsibility for all areas of our life, the more we thrive. Confidence and self-esteem are the natural consequences of knowing you can rely on your own good judgment. It's extremely powerful to learn to trust yourself and your ability to determine your next steps.

The New Therapy Paradigm

We want to take a moment here to stress that we don't disagree with psychotherapy or talk therapy. We are therapists after all! Instead, we believe that therapy is evolving. Just as the perspective of therapy has expanded to be a helpful tool for a wide-range of issues, so too must therapy itself evolve and expand.

So, what does this new therapy paradigm look like? We believe that therapy must expand to be more YOU-focused. This is where that ambition and motivation we talked about at the beginning of this chapter comes into play. Instead of showing up to a therapy session for an hour a week and relying on the techniques your psychotherapist suggests, we want you to be in the driver's seat. We believe that the greatest transformations happen when you're guided through exercises and techniques that you work on independently. In this way, you are in control of and experience your own progress. This self-directed process offers greater, long-lasting impact because it's personalized, internally resourced and guided by your intuition.

In the end, you are the power behind the change. When you sit with yourself, explore the emotions behind your thoughts and actions, and then actively work to re-create the experiences and imprint positive change, you're not just healing old wounds, you're learning how to trust yourself. That's an invaluable lesson that we can't stress the importance of enough.

The awareness, confidence, and courage that will manifest in your life because of practicing self-guided techniques will show up in everything you do. What's more, the impact will be sustainable and deep because this methodology gives you the chance to change your brain. We're not just talking about the way you think or feel; we're talking actual, physical changes to the brain that influence your thoughts, feelings, and perspective.

Tracy Zboril and Cara Hewett

CHAPTER 2: YOU CAN CHANGE YOUR BRAIN

You might have heard of the term neuroplasticity, but if you haven't, don't worry, because it's exactly what we're going to be talking about in this chapter. We mentioned in Chapter 1 that it's one thing to temporarily change the way you think or feel, but it's another altogether to make physical changes to your brain that, in turn, affect the way you think and feel. Those changes are possible because of neuroplasticity, and this recent discovery, that the brain is malleable, is a huge game-changer for the field of psychotherapy. We personally consider it to be the holy grail of the human experience because it means that we have far more control over our behavior, our perspective, and even our destiny, than we once believed.

If that sounds far-fetched, keep in mind that neuroplasticity is not a theory; scientists have been able to prove that it's exactly how the brain functions. It is constantly adjusting and changing itself based on all the data it receives. Much of that data comes in the form of thoughts and feelings. In other words, when you change your thoughts and feelings, you change the physical structure of the brain.

Thought leaders in the areas of neuroscience, those measuring energy fields, those studying consciousness, and those researching the mind, body connection, are proving we can literally rewire our minds. You've probably heard about a lizard's pretty neat trick of regenerating its tail when it's cut off. We humans, of course, are unable to grow a new hand if one of ours is unfortunately severed, but until very recently, it was believed that we were entirely unable to regenerate at all, meaning that the cells in our brain were unable to re-grow once they died. The good news is, that old model was wrong. It has been discovered that our brain can indeed generate new cells.

It's not automatic, though. It requires work, concentration, and focus. That's why mindfulness and meditation are becoming so popular. When you learn any new skill, new neural pathways are formed. Anytime you want to form a new behavior or habit, to make it stick, you simply need to grow a new set of neural pathways. The new behavior will become a physical part of your brain, a new and very genuine, physical part of you. This is incredibly exciting information.

The Science Behind Re-Wiring Your Brain

Let's move into the how and why this takes place. To understand what neuroplasticity means, you'll first need to understand a few terms.

Neuron – a special cell that receives, transmits and processes information in your brain

Synapse – the space in between neurons where information fires. Imagine a neuron as a sparkler. The space at the end of the sparkler, where the sparks will fly when it's lit, is the synapse.

Neural Pathway – a connection between two neurons that is created when two synapses fire at the same time.

Don't worry if this doesn't make sense just yet. It will all come together soon, and you'll see how your brain is constructed, and most importantly, how it can easily be changed!

Let's first look at the term neuroplasticity. As you can see, it is made up of the words "neuro(n)" and "plasticity," which means it's the study of neurons' malleable properties of plastic, or, in other words, neurons' ability to change. This term, neuroplasticity, refers to the brain's potential to reorganize by creating new neural pathways to adapt as it sees fit.

Hebb's Law, a neuropsychological theory dating back to 1949, provides one of the cornerstone principles in understanding neuroplasticity and the powers of the mind. As stated by D.O. Hebb in *The Organization of Behavior*, "Neurons that fire together, wire together."

As John Kehoe, author of *Quantum Warriors,* states, "Neuroplasticity describes a very simple process. It refers to the ability of neurons to always forge new connections. Neuroplasticity at its essence is the process of the brain wiring and rewiring itself."

This re-wiring means that your brain is constantly creating neural pathways. It's these neural pathways that create habits and patterns of thinking and behavior. Neural pathways become connected in the brain when synapses fire together. Skills that are practiced repetitively cause larger and larger masses of neural connections to form in representation of these activities. This explains why practice (of anything) enables us to learn and then retain new skills. When we learn new behaviors, we actually alter the anatomy of the brain.

Many established behavioral theories in the field of psychology have stated that habits are formed through repetition over a period of about 30 days. Even though scientists could observe the outcomes consistently enough to draw conclusions about it, they still didn't understand the reasoning behind it. Scientists can now measure this synaptic reaction within the brain using PET scans and MRI scanning technology.

This relatively new information about the brain's neuroplasticity was instrumental in the development of our understanding of how we can really change the way we think. Before this discovery, we in the field of mental health did not recognize that we could reconfigure the brain as needed. We believed that medication was necessary to chemically alter the brain. In fact, creating neural pathways requires no medication at all. It happens naturally with every thought, emotion, action, and reaction.

How Neuroplasticity Affects You

This might seem pretty abstract at the moment, so we're going to walk you through a practical example that shows exactly how neural pathways are formed and how they affect behavior and vice versa.

The brain is always seeking to validate its experience. In other words, the brain operates by searching for information within itself to confirm the reality it's experiencing. This makes everything so much easier for us. For example, when we turn our hot shower on, we know that the water will be hot. We don't have to wonder or analyze how to make it so; in fact, we don't even think about it. That's a very simple example, but this automatic thought, perspective and behavior happens because your brain is always validating its experience. It is able to validate its experience because you've strengthened the neural pathways around that experience through repetitive behavior. Every day you turn on your hot shower, you strengthen that connection.

It's great that we don't have to walk around thinking about all the million tiny circumstances in our life that occur every second, but does the brain operate in the same way on a bigger scale? It does! So, let's look at the famous golfer Tiger Woods to understand how neuroplasticity works on the large scale.

It can be assumed, from a neuroscientific perspective, that in the height of his career, Tiger's brain had programmed neural pathways consisting of perfect golf swings. These neural pathways had been strengthened since childhood through intense, repetitive practice. From the small details like putting on his golf clothes or riding out on a golf cart, to actually holding a club and swinging, his brain was validating its experience and firing up the parts that knew exactly how to perform the perfect swing.

So, what happened? At some point, Tiger stopped making perfect swings, as is demonstrated by the decline in his career. But if his brain was programmed to make perfect swings, how could he begin to falter? Something disrupted those neural pathways. In other words, at some point during his repetitive practice, a change was made, and it's possible that his negative, emotional, and personal experiences off the field were the source. If his focus was altered by those personal experiences, he would have been forming new neural pathways that related to the personal experiences rather than strengthening the perfect swing connections.

Of course, this is all theoretical because we don't know what was going on inside Tiger Woods' brain, but his decline does serve as an excellent example of how neural pathways are built, maintained, and then can be disrupted. This applies to both negative and positive experiences because the brain doesn't distinguish between the two. It merely receives the information and either forms a new connection or strengthens or disrupts an existing one. So, you can form positive habits and break negative ones just as easy.

Applying Neuroplasticity to Your Life

Neuroplasticity, as it applies to behavior and thought, is a revolutionary discovery. Your inner monologue, unhealthy habits, automatic reactions, and even your fears, doubts, and insecurities are all hard-wired into your brain through neural pathways, but these neural pathways aren't permanent. They can be changed, and healthier reactions and habits can take their place.

It's not as easy as simply thinking or acting differently. Some of these pathways in your brain were created a long time ago, and they've been reinforced for decades. If repeating a positive thought could address these stronger pathways, then positive affirmations and CBT (Cognitive Behavioral Therapy) would be all you need. But as you know by now, our experience tells us otherwise. When it comes to really changing these pathways, you need access to the source.

So, what's the block between consciously thinking differently and really changing the neural pathways in your brain? The brain absolutely can change, but to really be effective, much of that change needs to happen in the subconscious. When neural pathways become so strong that our behaviors and actions are automatic, they're housed in the subconscious, and to change them, you must gain access that part of the mind.

Accessing the subconscious might sound like a daunting task, but it's quite easy. Much of the work needed to make changes to even lifelong habits can be done while consciously accessing the subconscious, or in other words, working on the border between the two. Later, we'll dive more in-depth into how to work with the subconscious mind, but in brief, here are a few effective methods:

Slowing brain wave frequencies – Occurs during deep states of meditation, facilitating practice of quieting the mind-chatter, allowing for focus and concentration.

Creative visualization - Using detailed imagery to create new experiences, real or imagined.

Evoking emotion - The mind uses the language of the senses to let us feel emotions in our body. We can induce an emotional state by concentrating on these sensations.

Repetition – The mind forms connections through repetition, which eventually leads into automatic behavior and the subconscious mind.

The technique we developed uses a few different exercises similar to the ones mentioned above to gain access to the deeply ingrained neural pathways in the subconscious mind. The next few chapters will detail the research behind these techniques, but first, let's take a deeper look into the subconscious mind, how it stores memories, and how that affects our emotional wellbeing.

Tracy Zboril and Cara Hewett

CHAPTER 3: UNDERSTANDING THE SUBCONSCIOUS MIND

In the last dozen years, great strides in the field of neuroscience have revealed that the root of problematic behavior lies within the part of our mind known as the subconscious. Long before advanced imaging technology, Freud correctly described our minds as an iceberg, where the visible tip we see above water is our conscious mind, and the behemoth beneath the surface is the subconscious. Our subconscious mind might feel small because it works on autopilot, but it makes up the vast majority of our consciousness.

The subconscious is the intuitive part of us that acts without our conscious awareness. It's the part that behaves naturally and freely in any given situation. When we're able to bypass the critical, analytical mind (conscious mind) the subconscious mind becomes free to work intuitively. Changes that are made from this subconscious part of the brain can be sustainable and long-lasting because they aren't hindered by the conscious mind questioning and reanalyzing each situation that arises.

Your Subconscious is Always Aware

Because of the nature of the subconscious and its absence of critical thinking, it can be easily influenced. One way to understand this is to look at the media and how they use this feature to their advantage. When you hear the phrase "subliminal message," it might sound like a conspiracy theory, but this type of hidden advertising is constantly at play. From billboards to TV commercials to magazines and radio ads, hidden messaging serves to sneak ideas past the conscious mind. This can be accomplished in several ways like quietly repeated phrases or words hidden within pictures. Your conscious mind might not be paying attention, but your subconscious is always aware, taking everything in. It is always listening, so even when you don't notice those hidden messages, your mind still receives the information and stores it.

Since your subconscious is always alert, it's constantly receiving billions of bits of information. Just look around you right now and try to notice how many words, colors, shapes, sounds, and smells are vying for your attention. Even if you're in a quiet room, there's still so much information to receive. That would obviously be overwhelming for your conscious mind, so it's a good thing your subconscious can take this on for you.

But if the subconscious is constantly alert, how does information get prioritized? This process happens in several ways, but one of the shortcuts is through your senses. Our senses are key for our survival, so any piece of information that stimulates or makes the promise of stimulating the senses gets marked as priority. Again, the media is keenly aware of this, and they use it. For example, a drink advertisement might flash the word "thirsty" in the background to signal your subconscious to feel thirst. Have you ever wandered to the freezer to look for ice cream after seeing a Dairy Queen commercial? There is no coincidence there. Your subconscious pays attention to everything, and it takes special note of sensory messaging.

The power of advertising really comes down to a combination of three key factors, two of which we've already discussed: using subliminal messaging to move past the conscious mind and utilizing the senses to flag the messages as priority. The third factor is taking advantage of brain wave states. Most advertising works because of your relaxed state of mind while watching TV, listening to the radio, or driving. These activities induce a certain brain wave state that makes your subconscious more suggestible. The more entranced you are in an activity, the more open your subconscious is to influence. While watching television or a movie, your brain wave frequencies slow down; you are focused, alert and aware. This creates the perfect scenario to see a frosty chunk of vanilla ice cream blended in slow motion with luscious pieces of chocolate.

It might feel sneaky and a little uncomfortable that advertisers use these techniques to influence your purchasing decisions. While the ethics of that are a discussion for another book, we only brought up this example to illustrate how powerful your subconscious mind is. By simply getting into a certain state or brain wave and then utilizing your senses, you can influence how you think and feel. This is the very foundation of hypnosis, and it's also part of the technique we're discussing in this book.

Using Hypnosis to Access the Subconscious

Brain waves states and the concepts associated with hypnosis are not new. In fact, hypnosis has been around since the late 1800's. Unfortunately, it received a bad rap from circus shows where people were mesmerized into quacking like a duck on stage, in part because of pioneering hypnotist Franz Mesmer (the word "mesmerize" stems from his name). This showman used a cape and a wand and gave hypnosis the reputation of being associated with the occult.

Over the years, the reputation of hypnosis has changed. While some performers still use hypnosis as a form of entertainment, and some associate it with government conspiracy, it has become a useful, professional tool in the field of psychology. The benefits of hypnosis are profound, and those effects have been backed up through scientific studies. In fact, imaging and EEGs (a test that displays the electrical activity of the brain) have proven that hypnosis does indeed slow down brain waves, and in turn, makes the subject more suggestible. These slowed down brain waves, like those found in meditation, elicit focus and concentration. Not only are we more easily influenced in this state, but we learn faster and lessons learned have more longevity.

Dr. Joe Dispenza, through his research using EEG scans, has shed great light on this subject with his neuroscientific research. He is truly a pioneer in the field as it relates to using brain wave frequencies for self-healing of the emotional and physical body. His research concludes that feelings completely bypass our conscious mind and go directly into our subconscious where chemicals associated with the corresponding feeling are released. For example, fear will produce the stress hormone, cortisol.

He explains how to do this by shedding light on the placebo process. While we might think of placebos as a mental trick, in reality, it's a scientific process where our brains produce chemicals associated with feelings. In other words, whatever we believe is happening is what our brain reacts to. So, we can actually produce helpful, peaceful chemicals in the brain and form new, strong neural connections by simply feeling peace, gratitude, and compassion. Dispenza further explains that getting your brain into a calm state, or a hypnotic state, increases your ability to create these hormones.

Understanding Brain Waves

Your brain operates at different frequency levels, or vibrations. The faster the vibration, the more conscious you are. As that vibration slows and the frequency lowers, you gain more access to the subconscious mind. Because this is so important to the method we're discussing, let's take a more in depth look at brain wave activity.

As you read this book, you are in the brainwave frequency called "beta." You are in the present moment, and you have an increased alertness, concentration, and cognition. In alpha, the next brain wave frequency, the activity is slowed down, and you experience an increase in relaxation, visualization, and creativity. When you're truly relaxed, and the brainwaves are slower, you're in a reduced state of consciousness where awareness can expand. More simply put, when the body relaxes, the mind expands, allowing for greater imagination and creativity.

Though relaxed in the alpha state, you are fully conscious. You slip in and out of alpha throughout your day. For example, have you ever driven somewhere, found yourself deep in thought, gotten to your destination and realized you barely remember the drive? You were so preoccupied that your subconscious mind took over and pushed your conscious mind out of the driver's seat without you even knowing it. That might sound dangerous, but it's actually a helpful and completely safe state of mind because your subconscious knows exactly what to do when you are on autopilot.

While the driving example is the easiest for most of us to relate to, it stands to reason that any time you can get your conscious mind out of the way - the one that loves to analyze and judge - you will give your wiser subconscious mind the freedom to show you the way.

This is why athletic coaches have begun training their athletes to stay in alpha. If a tennis player is emotionally reacting to the last bad shot, he will likely miss the next one. But if that player can stay in alpha and allow autopilot to kick in, he can avoid the trap of judging and overanalyzing. The next shot is successfully made because the athlete's subconscious mind has been trained to know exactly how to perform that shot.

Many of today's professional golfers have mastered staying in alpha for entire holes, from the drive to the putt. Golf is such a mental game and breaking out of alpha gets the critical mind engaged and can truly break one's stride. We mentioned Tiger Woods' golf game in a previous chapter, but one thing we didn't talk about is that at the top of his game, he was perceived as impersonal on the field. He was often criticized for this because he didn't stop to shake hands or make eye contact or smile at the spectators. This likely had nothing to do with his personality or temperament, but probably everything to do with his state of mind and focus. Some sports psychologists refer to this as being in "the zone." Staying in alpha mode, even between holes, protects this state of mind and doesn't allow anything to break that autopilot brain frequency.

The Subconscious is an Active Memory Bank

Now that you understand a little more about what the subconscious is and a few ways it can be accessed and used to influence your behavior, let's talk about the type of data your subconscious holds onto. This is important information because it's going to help you understand the function of all those neural pathways we talked about in Chapter 2.

To illustrate how our mind holds onto feelings and data, we're going to tell you about a previous client of Cara's named Amy. In her mid-thirties, Amy was seeking therapy to try to raise her self-esteem. Although Amy was a physically beautiful woman, she was plagued with years of insecurity about her appearance. Therapeutic techniques included coming up with a list of positive statements that represented how she hoped to view herself, such as, "I am beautiful," "I exude confidence and charm," "People are drawn to me," etc.

Amy was given the assignment to state the list of ten positive affirmations, daily, in front of the mirror, ten times during the morning and ten times during the evening. She was also asked to repeat them during her therapy sessions.

During one of these sessions, Amy crumbled up her list, threw it, and exclaimed, "This is ridiculous! I feel like an idiot stating these things that simply are not true for me."

It was understood that, over time, with enough repetition, she would begin to believe the statements she was making about herself. After all, this is basic Cognitive Behavioral Therapy, the go-to form of talk therapy. And repetitive self-statements of positive affirmations were (and still are) the treatment of choice for changing thoughts. But Amy continued to practice her affirmations to no avail.

Why weren't the affirmations working? Just like we discussed in Chapter 2, repetition could change the neural pathways that were at the root of her insecurities, but if her insecurity was so strongly and deeply held in the subconscious, it would automatically negate simple affirmations. She would need to access those deep-rooted beliefs first before positive repetitions could be effective. This is where CBT often fails to make long-lasting change. It can be helpful in some circumstances, but our experience as therapists showed us that some beliefs are so deeply engrained in the subconscious, that only by accessing them and changing them at their root can a client really experience healing.

When the cognitive dissonance - the distance between the desired belief and the current belief - is too great, the insurmountable incongruity renders these forms of treatment ineffective. In hindsight, it would have been better to address Amy's insecurity issues differently. Now we know that a more effective path would have been to initially focus on the subconscious mind where her feelings of insecurity existed as they clung to relevant memories.

Like Amy, we all have some degree of unwanted emotional baggage we're carrying around. What do you tell yourself throughout the day? Is it a litany of negative self-talk? As you go through your day, are you attempting to keep up appearances? Is there a disconnect between what you really feel and what you present to the outer world?

Don't get discouraged by your answers to those questions. If you've never worked directly with the root of your negative emotions stored in the subconscious mind, then you're likely to find the associated insecurities and fears creeping up in your daily life. Our minds tend to cling on to the negative, making us feel like the walking wounded. The good news is, it doesn't matter how old or deep these wounds are, they can be healed.

CHAPTER 4: THE WALKING WOUNDED

We all have memory banks chock-full of past failures, disappointments, and negative beliefs that we've stored away over time. Those negative beliefs have formed because of our experiences. Those experiences produced emotions and it's those emotions that are the real culprits in lodging painful memories in our subconscious minds. In this chapter, we're going to detail the origins of how this all happens to us - how we develop fears and insecurities. Then, we'll show you how these negatively charged memories can dissipate, quickly and easily.

Just as we discussed in the last chapter, the deep insecurities, fears, and emotions lodged in the subconscious mind are the automated blocks that can keep you from moving forward. When you're able to directly address those blocks, you can clear away the negative emotion and make rapid progress toward creating new neural pathways. First, let's take a look at how all that negativity gets stored in the first place.

We've all got Clusters

We have accumulated all our experiences - both negative and positive within our subconscious. The negative and emotionally charged memories tend to be stickier than benign or positive experiences. This might seem unfortunate at first, but when you think about it, it's a great survival tool. We're built to remember the negative, so we can protect ourselves from it in the future. The problem arises as these experiences build up over time and clog the system. We refer to this as a cluster. Clusters tend to accumulate up front, take up space and override positive memories.

Clusters form around an emotion, whether it be fear, anger, humiliation or something equally unpleasant. That cluster gets triggered when something similar happens and then floods you with the same emotion and can interfere with your day-to-day dealings. These emotional hijackings take place in all areas of our lives. They can happen in our workplaces and in our marriages, friendships, families, and parenting practices. How many times have any of us - responsible, good-hearted people - walked away from a situation, embarrassed and wondering why we responded so poorly to a negative situation.

To illustrate this point, we want to tell you about our client, Cathy. Cathy is a successful, driven career-woman who was dealing with a trauma that left her feeling insecure. While undergoing a difficult divorce that took up much of her time and left her emotionally drained and preoccupied, she was fired from a large account. It was the first time she'd been fired from an account in her 20-year career. For the first time ever, Cathy began to question her own abilities. Self-doubt started creeping into all her other business dealings until she found herself deeply questioning her own talent and expertise. Even though Cathy continued to have many successful ongoing business accounts, this one "failure" was all she could focus on.

Her subconscious mind was holding onto this particular memory and it was interfering with her ability to break through the cluster stored up front in her memory bank. This one failed business incident had attached itself to the energy of the other accumulated gunk, making up that cluster - past failures and disappointments, leading all the way back to her childhood. The point we're making here is that one incident can trigger emotions rooted in old trauma we don't even realize we are carrying with us. This explains why we can overreact to situations and have no idea where those emotional outbursts come from.

We are the Walking Wounded

Through our research, we've realized the magnitude of the effect that trauma (at any level) has and how it interferes with our lives. All our present-day behaviors are the direct result of past trauma we're still carrying around in our subconscious minds. Every single one of us is a walking-wounded human. No one is exempt. Some of us have experienced more trauma than others, but the underlying effect is the same for us all. Our default setting, as a result, is fear.

The emotion of fear paralyzes us. Our past disappointments and failures that are stored away in our subconscious are like wounds that never fully heal. The wounds might temporarily scab over and seem less significant, but they're always vulnerable to being reopened whenever something with a similar energy to the original wounding pops up again. Throughout life, we're triggered by any negative experiences that mirror the kind of fear that initially created the stored trauma. The new experience gets filtered through the cluster and the wound is reopened, often causing us to respond with more emotional energy than the current situation warrants.

According to leading transpersonal theorist Dr. Paul Masters, psychologists estimate that 9/10 of the conscious reactions people have to events in their daily lives, from the most trivial to major occurrences, are based upon what they have come to *expect*. These expectations are fed to the conscious mind as computer-like feedback from the subconscious memory bank. In order to move beyond the negative emotional blocks preventing you from moving forward in life, the subconscious mind must be cleared of the cluster.

It's important to keep in mind that this is simply how the subconscious mind takes in information, reacts to it, then directs the involuntary nervous system, setting up a chain of physical responses. That is why we, the walking wounded, feel out of control when in the grip of any strong emotion, whether it's fear, anger, rage, or sadness.

To continue the wound analogy, imagine that this wound gets reopened and scabs over numerous times throughout life. At some point, the scab becomes so hard and thick you no longer recognize it. Without even realizing it, you have assimilated the emotion of fear. The fear then becomes part of your make-up, your personality.

Here's an example: Sally, a highly competent and experienced public speaker, receives a bad review from a workshop participant, and the negative energy of this business trauma gets stored in her subconscious.

Though she was always previously poised and confident, Sally goes into her next workshop as a walking wounded, filled with apprehension.

The event goes exceptionally well. But at the end of the seminar, as the participants are given the feedback forms, Sally feels the emotion of fear surfacing. The original wound is being reopened. The longer she watches the participants provide feedback, the more her anxiety builds. The current situation is being filtered through the debris of the stored trauma.

Eventually, Sally succumbs to a full-blown panic attack. Through her embarrassment and shock, this quintessential pro looks around and wonders if anyone can tell that her heart is racing, she's short of breath, and sweat is pouring down her face. This is a classic example of the walking wounded.

We can never underestimate the effects of traumatic experiences on our lives. One career related trauma started to unravel Sally's professional confidence level. And this is a natural response. There is nothing wrong with it. Sally is reacting according to how our minds operate, and no one is immune.

You Subconscious is an Overflowing Storage Unit

Let's expand on this some more. We start forming memories around the age of three. From that time on, memories are stored in our subconscious mind. Over time, we have a huge inventory, as you can imagine. The negative memories stay in the forefront in an accumulated pile of debris. For us to perform optimally in our lives, this pile of negative memories needs to be cleared out.

How does this work? You can rapidly download an unimaginable amount of data as it comes at you. It all gets stored in your memory bank. Think of it as a huge computer storage unit. Your evolved intellectual mind can retrieve anything in the data storage unit. You call this retrieval process "remembering." But, a lot of the data you've stored throughout your life is mundane and unnecessary. This data gets pushed further and further back into the unit.

Let's dive into the subconscious a little more. Can you remember what you had for dinner last night? Good; what was it? Did you remember it by seeing a picture of it? The subconscious works through the senses, and in this case, it utilized your visual sense. Did you know that you can retrieve what you had for dinner the second Tuesday in March in second grade? It's in there. Your mind simply doesn't bother retrieving that information because it's not important. It's buried under all that other data, way far back in the memory storage unit. But what you ate last night is still in front.

Now, here's where things run amuck. Memories of intense experiences that provoke intense feelings - great fear, sadness, humiliation, even happiness - remain stored at the front of the storage unit even after many years have passed.

Since the memories of your most intensely-felt moments are right at the forefront, their energy can easily be re-activated. Whenever a new event in your life conjures up feelings, like the feelings you were having when these prior memories were created, you will likely experience emotion that seems out of proportion to the current circumstance. The new event has re-activated the stored trauma from the prior similar event.

For instance, if you were attacked by a dog early in your childhood, even if you don't consciously remember the incident, it's likely that dogs will bring up intense fear for you. The stored memory of that childhood trauma will re-activate your fear, even in current, safe instances around dogs where fear is not called for.

If you are a woman who was abandoned by her father at a very early age, you have stored an intense memory that feels like abandonment. It would not be unusual for you to become a woman with an irrational fear of abandonment by men, even though the men in your adult life have nothing to do with the original stored memory.

Primitive vs. Evolved Brain

Let's talk now about the primitive brain and the more evolved brain. To understand this, we're going to compare our brains to animals. Obviously, we know that we are different from animals in many ways. This is because we have both a primitive and evolved brain. Animals exclusively have a primitive brain that dictates their survival. Our brains also have this primitive brain, but it is contained in our much larger, evolved brain. So, we do still have the same survival instincts as animals, but unlike them, our survival instincts are layered with complex memories, emotions, and critical thoughts.

The best way to understand how the primitive and evolved brain works is to share an example of an animal whose life is being threatened. In this case, let's look at what happens to a rabbit. Imagine a rabbit nibbling away in his favorite cabbage patch. Suddenly, a fox approaches and as soon as the rabbit becomes aware of the fox, he has an immediate sensation of fear. On a biological level, his body is flooded with adrenaline and cortisol, giving him the strength and energy to run for his life. He does not make the conscious decision to run. It is simply an instinct – a sensation that triggers a flood of hormones appropriate to the situation. This is the primitive brain at work.

Once he reaches the safety of his little rabbit hole, the feeling of fear turns off like a switch. The rabbit doesn't sit and analyze his performance. He doesn't criticize himself for the path he took or the speed at which he ran. No, that rabbit won't have another thought or feeling until another action is required. As he begins to feel the sensation of hunger, he then takes the action to go find food. As he once again approaches the cabbage patch, he feels no trepidation about the fox incident. If it's not currently happening, he does not remember it.

Our primitive brain reacts in the same way. A sensation triggers a response that causes a flood of the appropriate hormones to prepare the body for whatever action it might need to take. This is often called the flight, fight, faint, or feign response. In other words, when you need to survive, your critical mind shuts off and your body gives you the necessary hormones to run, fight, hide, or submit. Again, this is not a conscious choice. Your brain makes these decisions in an instant without your awareness, and the next thing you know, you're feeling incredibly angry, energetic, afraid, or even numb.

It's our evolved brains and our ability to critically think that complicates this instinct. While we do react in order to survive, based on the circumstances around us, we also have the clusters we discussed earlier in this chapter that influence our actions and reactions. We can get triggered into a survival response, even when our life isn't in danger. This is because of the way we store and process memories. A primitive brain doesn't hold all the connections that an evolved brain does. Its storage vault is smaller and less complex. Our evolved brain means our storage unit of memories is infinite and has a very detailed filing system. Our reactions and instincts are pulled from the data within that storage system. Instead of simply reacting to a moment, we react to past situations associated with the present moment.

Let's look at this difference by returning to our example of the rabbit. He just takes the memory of his encounter with the fox, stores it, and doesn't analyze it. He will go back to the cabbage patch again when he is hungry. Over time, if the fox continues to appear, he might accumulate enough data to decide that particular cabbage patch is unsafe, and then seek out another one. But even so, he won't approach all cabbage patches with paranoia and fear. His brain will simply retrieve relevant data points and inspire action accordingly.

If his brain were less primitive, he would begin to consciously analyze his experiences, and in doing so, would accumulate stored traumas that get triggered every time he sees a cabbage patch. He might then choose to numb his brain by smoking or overeating. This self-indulgent coping mechanism might then inspire feelings of guilt and shame, which then might trigger a feeling memory from childhood.

The point is, our primitive brains are responsible for our survival, but our evolved brains attach meaning to experiences and use our conscious minds to analyze and critically think about those experiences. Those experiences are then paired with other similar memories and the clusters begin to form and dictate our emotional responses.

The more intense the memory, the higher priority it gets in our memory banks. Those memories are stored up front in the storage unit where they are easily retrieved, then, when we have a situation that brings up a similar feeling, for instance, fear, our primitive (subconscious) immediately taps into the cluster (similar memories stored up front). The feelings of fear are intensified, and we overreact. All too often, when a current situation matches the feeling of a stored memory, we react disproportionately.

This is how memories can interfere with our ability to keep present-day events in their proper perspective. Sadly, we often take this problem one step further by projecting the fear into our future as well. That's a classic example of worry, and it causes the human mind and body considerable stress.

Here's an example: Let's say that every time you sit down in your car to drive somewhere, the images of a prior car accident pop into your mind, projecting the accident into your present by making you feel fearful. The more you drive with a sense of fear or dread, the better the chance you'll end up in another accident. That's a worst-case scenario, but at the very least, you've flooded your body with the stress hormone cortisol, and that, of course, causes all kinds of issues.

Cortisol levels build up in the blood, wreaking havoc on your mind and body. This way of thinking is the underlying cause of stress, anxiety, and depression. By truly living in the present, where the past and future do not exist, we can live our lives without angst. If we clear out all that debris in the memory bank, living in the past becomes a non-issue. Our technique works to do precisely that. We access the subconscious mind and then engage in exercises that clean up the stored memories. Healing on an emotional level takes place.

Heal The Wound at Its Roots

Because your trauma and memories and the associated responses are housed in your subconscious mind, that's where the healing needs to take place. If you exclusively work with the conscious mind, you won't be able to access the patterns that guide your automatic reactions. The key to healing the wounds is to use your conscious mind to guide the healing of your subconscious. In other words, you can use the advantages of your evolved brain to change the programming that's causing your primitive brain to overreact.

Utilizing concepts related to NeuroLinguistic Programing, we now know how to clear or scramble the complex memories that trigger your primitive brain, so that they do not carry the emotional magnitude they once did. One this healing takes place, you have the ability to use your innate guidance systems to effectively and consistently generate self-confidence, peacefulness, and a strong reliance on your own inner knowing.

Remember Cathy from the beginning of the chapter? She had a setback in her career after being fired from an account during her divorce. This caused a spiral of insecurity, anxiety and was affecting her career and personal life. We were able to use clearing exercises to minimize the intensity of the original trauma. The one failure was finally put in its proper perspective and bumped out of its primary position, relegated to the recesses of the memory bank along with similar, less potent disappointments and failures. The memories were not gone; they were just no longer interfering, allowing Cathy to feel as though she was back on her game.

Cathy was able to find her confidence again because she stopped the cycle of automatic reactions. The complex connections between her recent divorce, business failure, and related insecurities were healed by being placed appropriately in her evolved brain. That might sound like an intense and complicated process, but it really is as simple as accessing the right part of the brain and then healing the wounds at their roots using proven techniques.

CHAPTER 5: LET'S TALK ABOUT MANIFESTATION

You're more than likely familiar with the concepts of manifestation in one way or another, whether it's through *The Secret* or *The Law of Attraction*. The idea that your thoughts manifest the reality around you has become a big piece of pop culture and new age beliefs. The mainstream appeal on the topic is mostly rooted in rags to riches stories, where someone visualized a car, house or new job, and then it manifested in their life. While this is one aspect of manifestation, there are deeper principles at work here and understanding those principles is an important part of the technique we're discussing in this book.

In this chapter, we're going to look at manifestation, but more importantly, we're going to discuss the scientific principles at work behind its power. Rather than looking at manifestation through the lens of new age systems, we will look at it through a microscope, a scientific viewpoint that validates its existence with evidence. Much of this research is focused on energy and quantum physics, so we'll discuss the basic principles behind these subjects and then explain how they apply to the Soul Happy technique.

The point we really want to drive home is that manifestation isn't just about attracting your desires through focused, active thought. As we've discussed in the last few chapters, long-lasting change happens by using your conscious mind to access your subconscious through calm brain wave states that allow you to heal wounds and break up clusters at their roots. Remaining in the conscious mind alone impedes your ability to deeply heal.

Along those lines, we also want to point out that much of what we'll cover in this chapter relates back to the principles of neuroplasticity that we discussed in Chapter 2. If you can change your brain, you can change your thoughts and reactions. It stands to reason that doing so will also change your perspective and therefore, your reality.

Often, in the discussion on manifestation, the concept of neuroplasticity and the principles behind working with the subconscious mind are left out. In this chapter, we're going to work to fill in those gaps. While this might be the most science-heavy chapter, we're going to approach this discussion practically and make sure you understand why it's important and how you can use it to change your brain and heal yourself. Let's start by looking at the foundation of manifestation – energy.

Everything is Energy

Most are aware that all things are made of energy, both seen and unseen. This is not a new concept. Thought leaders, philosophers and scientists all around the world have been saying as much for years, and in our recent history, we've been able to prove the theory through advanced imaging technology. We all accept this as truth, but it can be a hard concept to grasp fully as a reality.

For instance, if you examine your hand right now, you'll see it as a solid object, but in reality, there are billons and billions of tiny electrons buzzing around and bumping into or being repelled away from each other. Those moments of attraction and repulsion are what create the solid form. On the smallest level, we are simply energy, but we're not colliding into each other or melting into the floor because the energy field created by certain electrons refuses to collide with the energy field of another.

It's still a hard concept to grasp, but it might help to think of electrons as little tornados swirling around the nucleus of an atom. That fast, swirling motion creates waves of vibrational energy. When you zoom into those atoms, you'd see extremely fast-moving electrons, but when you zoom out, you see the collective of every atom that eventually creates a solid object.

Whether you're able to conceptualize this or not, the most important takeaway is that everything, at its smallest level, is vibrating energy. That includes every living thing and every non-living thing. From the chair you're sitting in to the air you're breathing – it's all vibrating energy. Remember from Chapter 2 that thoughts are actually electrical synapses firing in your brain, so even your thoughts and emotions, at their core, are vibrating energy.

You might have been able to grasp this concept of energy in regard to solid objects, but it might be even more of a challenge to apply it to things invisible to the human eye. To help you understand this, imagine listening to the radio. The song, the electric signal operating the radio, the radio frequency being received, and the information being processed by your ears is all invisible to you, but you know it exists. If it exists, you know that it's energy. So, try to keep in mind that when we're talking about your thoughts and emotions, your subconscious and conscious mind, we're still talking about something that, at its core, is vibrational energy.

Energy is Easily Influenced

Now that you have at least a basic understanding that there is an energetic composition of everything seen and unseen, let's look at how this energy operates. For the purposes of this discussion, we're going to focus specifically on the energy within and around the body and mind. Ancient knowledge has long contended that there is an auric field within and around or body that can be influenced and changed through focus and meditation. Neuroscientific research has now confirmed that our emotional and physical well-being is directly influenced by these energy pathways. Science has even measured and documented this energy.

Modern thought leaders, who also happen to be western medical doctors, like Dr. Oz, Dr. Chopra, and Dr. Dispenza, are discovering more and more about this mind-body connection. For example, in Dr. Chopra's, book, *Reinventing the Body, Resurrecting the Soul*, he contends that every cell is made up of two invisible ingredients: awareness and energy. His book relays the steps to harness those basic elements to change the distorted energy patterns that are the root cause of aging, infirmity, and disease. We maintain that this same process can be used for the purposes of transforming your emotional state and well-being as well.

Not only are there exciting discoveries in the field of neuroscience; but recent findings by bio-geneticists compliment and confirm the same theory that energy can be influenced by your mind. In another book by Dr. Chopra, co-authored with Rudolph Tanzi Ph.D, *Super Genes*, they postulate that even our genetic coding is comprised of impressionable energy. For decades, medical science has believed that genes determine our biological destiny and remain unchanged. But, the authors argue that our genes are dynamic and responsive to everything we think, say, and do. Through Dr. Chopra's studies, they are finding that the human body is far more capable of healing and renewal than anyone suspected.

According to research by Joe Dispenza, these fields of energy are measurable. He attests that the moment we send energy into our heart by allowing ourselves to deeply feel joy, gratitude, compassion, the field of energy around our body expands to nine meters wide. Conversely, living in fear and sadness causes your energy field to shrink. He argues that the heart has a magnetic field that sends out ripples of energy, like the way dropping a pebble in water sends out ripples in all directions. The more you can be in that heart-centered state, the more pebbles you are dropping in the water. The more ripples you send out to create, to manifest, to deliver the information of your intentions, the more impact you have on your life and the world.

All these discoveries, of which we've hardly scratched the surface in covering in this discussion, confirm that our thoughts, emotions, memories, and all the contents of the subconscious and conscious that we've been discussing in this book, aren't magical or inaccessible. Everything we've discussed and will continue to address in this book is merely energy that can be shifted and changed. When we talk about manifestation, in the context of Soul Happy, we're talking about the very real and proven ability to create positive patterns of thought and behavior. We can change our brain chemically, structurally and energetically.

Manifestation and Energy

To really grasp how all this ties together, let's revisit the electron and dive into a bit of quantum physics. Remember that the electron is the energetic basis of everything in our universe. They are the smallest manifestation of life, vibrating and creating the spark of everything that exists. You might be surprised to know that the creative powers of humankind, our thoughts and attention, directly affect the action of electrons. If that sounds spooky, you're not alone. Einstein termed the ability of one atom to affect another unrelated atom far across the universe, Spooky Action at a Distance. It seems unreal, but quantum reality, the reality that exists on the level of an electron, usually defies the logic and physics of the universe on a larger level.

Try to take that in for a moment – your thoughts can directly affect the action of an electron all the way across the universe, even on another planet or in the far reaches of space. Quantum physicists have even been able to determine that electrons and particles will behave completely differently when they're observed as opposed to when they're not. The mere process of paying attention to an electron can change its vibrational pattern and speed. If so much can change through simple observation, imagine what your intention and feelings can do.

There are plenty of books dedicated to explaining the concepts behind quantum theory, and while most of that information is far beyond the scope of this book, we want to make sure you understand that your thoughts and feelings are immensely powerful – they literally shape the world around you. You are constantly, in every second, creating the world you inhabit because your thoughts, intentions, observations, and feelings are influencing electrons, energy in its purest form.

It's important to note that this energy is not inherently negative or positive; it's completely neutral. Our thoughts are what qualify energy to manifest the electrons into form. How they are qualified by our thoughts determines their various shapes and densities, thus determining their form. In other words, electrons are called into action by our thoughts, positive or negative. They respond to both positivity and negativity without judgment, and their numbers and vibrations are determined accordingly, eventually repelling or attracting and creating form.

There's an infinite supply of electrons available for our creative powers. Since energy can neither be created or destroyed, intentionally using your thoughts and feelings makes you an alchemist, influencing the energy to create accordingly. Look at your life. Whatever you have created around you is a direct result of how you used these electrons through your thoughts, feelings and intentions.

Thoughts that stem from fear and anger have the same potential for attraction as thoughts that stem from love, joy and hope. The electrons are called to action either way. One version produces electrons accumulating together to form good in your life, the other negativity. Do you see that the electrons are neutral?

If you carry fear within yourself or if you think in a judging or self-doubting way toward others, the electrons of your own body will vibrate according to that negativity. They, in turn, will attract more negativity to these electrons whirling in your body where you hold the fear. This surmounting negativity can result in eventually creating disease, illness, depression, and aging.

On the other hand, thinking positively creates feelings of peacefulness and confidence. Those feelings then vibrate that energy and attract more positivity that matches their vibrational frequency. Positivity accumulates and creates circumstances, opportunities, health, and well-being that validate your confidence and sense of peace.

This cannot be overstated. Every time you have a thought or feeling, you send a vibration of energy, a frequency out into the world. This frequency aligns itself to other frequencies vibrating similarly, and it is through the alignment of these frequencies that the experience of your life is created - peaceful and harmonious, or otherwise. This is the foundation of manifestation – human thought and emotion attracting and repelling neutral electrons to vibrate in the same frequency.

Using Manifestation in the Soul Happy Technique

We've hammered the point home by now that conscious thought alone isn't enough to make long-lasting change. How does this coincide with what we've just discussed about manifestation? You might assume you'd be able to manifest your intentions simply with your desire, because your desire is entirely positive. You might assume that since you're not setting any intentions rooted in fear or anger, you should be golden. But that's just half the picture. All those small worries, fears, and doubts that crop up throughout the day - the ones that seem too benign and fleeting to worry about - those emotions are electron-based as well.

Electrons don't hand-pick the thoughts they respond to; it's their job to respond to *all* equally. We don't realize how much we sabotage our own great intentions until we become aware of all our fleeting worries and fear-based concerns throughout the day. This is why it's important to heal wounds at their roots and focus on subconscious and automatic patterns. Not only do those patterns block your ability to consciously make long-lasting change, they also attract electrons that match their vibration.

Those who have presented the laws of manifestation before us have failed to realize how effectively our stored emotional baggage can block our manifestation power. These buried, unexpressed emotions are the same unhealed energies that psychologists have been trying to help people clear for decades. The concepts you are discovering in these pages provides an understanding of how to go directly to the source - the subconscious - and remove these blocks. Removing emotional blocks, or separating from the emotional charge of the negative memories, allows for healing. Simply put, energy moves the blocks. So, what's the best route to accessing the information in the subconscious? That's the final piece of the puzzle that we're going to be looking at in the next chapter.

Tracy Zboril and Cara Hewett

CHAPTER 6: WORKING WITH THE RIGHT PART OF THE BRAIN

Access Your Subconscious

Now that you know the subconscious mind can be understood as energy that can be used for purposeful intention, the next trick is learning how to access it. To access and utilize the subconscious mind, you must first speak its language, which isn't English. We mentioned in Chapter 3 that sensory information causes the subconscious to flag incoming data as more important. This is the basis of the subconscious language – your senses - which is often spoken through, stories, metaphors and feelings.

In Chapter 3, we also discussed how brain waves act as gates to the subconscious mind – the higher the brain wave or faster the vibration, the more conscious you are, the slower the vibration, the more access you have to the subconscious. The sweet spot for accessing the subconscious is right below a state of mind called "the critical factor," where the conscious mind is active and disengaged from the subconscious. By lowering the brainwave to alpha, you are still aware, but you are focused and open to the subconscious mind. It's essentially the state between a fast-moving mind and a hypnotized one.

Dr. Joe Dispenza has measured the hormone serotonin and found it to be elevated in the alpha state. Serotonin is the hormone that gives you a sense of wellbeing, and when serotonin levels are low, depression, anxiety, and panic attacks are more prevalent. This is why mental health professionals and physicians are recognizing the benefits of meditation in combating stress. Slow the mind down, and your body chemistry changes. This has been validated in many university studies, including one at the University of Massachusetts Medical School. Dr. Deepak Chopra, has also studied, researched, and written many chapters on brain chemistry and the role of serotonin.

So, in order to access the subconscious, you need to speak its language by utilizing the senses and engaging in storytelling that evokes visualizations, feelings and sensations. You also need to be in a state of calm, right below the critical factor, but not too deeply disengaged that you end up in a state of hypnosis. Engaging both the conscious and subconscious mind together and working on the border between is the ideal spot for long-lasting transformation.

It's also important to note that the brain doesn't exclusively send signals to itself either; the heart does too. These signals also can influence perception, emotional experience, and higher mental processes. These signals have been identified and measured at the Heart Math Institute, where it was documented that the human heart emits an electromagnetic field that changes according to emotions. The heart sends more information to the brain than the brain sends to the heart. Not only have psychotherapists been working with the wrong part of the brain, but they've also completely missed the necessity of understanding the significance of the heart's influence.

Scientists at the Heart Math Institute also found that the heart has a system of neurons, and the signals they send to the brain can affect our emotional experiences. The information coming directly from the emotions being felt in your heart will inform the emotions being picked up by your brain, and they in turn will influence your perception of things. This happens instantaneously and without your knowledge.

In the techniques described in Part II, we will share with you many different ways to get into the ideal state of mind and speak the language of the subconscious. Some of these tools are used in the Soul Happy technique, while others are powerful devices that are not included in the technique, but are extremely effective at transforming the energy of the subconscious blocks.

Tying it All Together

To close out Part I, we want to tie together everything you've learned so far and solidify the importance of accessing the subconscious. This notion can be in contrast with many current schools of psychology that target the analytical, conscious mind. As talk therapists, we had spent decades attempting to get our clients to process feelings until they were no longer affected by them, but we found that it can take a *really* long time, when the conscious mind is constantly judging, questioning, and analyzing.

We recognized that the energy and time it takes to affect change from the conscious mind can also be a painful journey. As emotions are brought up for the purposes of "processing," re-experiencing the pain can sometimes be unbearable. And once relief is achieved, if ever, it can come back over time, as the conscious mind falls back into the old pattern of anger, sadness, or fear.

Thankfully, working with the deep-rooted memories of the subconscious is not as painful, because there is no need to bring the memories and feelings to the conscious mind in order to re-experience them. Instead, the work can be done directly where the memory is stored, eliminating the re-experiencing, and causing permanent change.

It is our hope that you now understand some important concepts that formed the foundation of the Soul Happy technique. In Part II, we'll take these concepts and show you how we practically apply them to each step in our technique. To review, here are the key concepts to take away from Part I.

- The most powerful change is self-directed change. Seeking expert advice is reasonable, but true change must be guided by intuition and judgment. Sustainable, long-lasting transformations can only happen when you do the work.

- Our brains are changeable, at a physical level. New neural pathways are being created all the time, and old ones are being reinforced or diminished. This knowledge helps us understand that we *can* change.

- Neural pathways are housed in the subconscious mind where all our experiences and memories are stored. To access the subconscious, you must change your brain waves, or state of mind, to a place of calmed focus.

- Strong emotions tend to stick in the subconscious, forming clusters. Those clusters are frequently triggered and incite a flood of emotions and thoughts that interfere with day-to-day life. These clusters must be broken up to incite long-lasting change.

- Once clusters are cleared, you can use the properties of energy to impress positive, healthy thoughts and habits into your subconscious mind, which will immediately affect your attitude, physical health, and the world around you.

PART II:

THE SOUL HAPPY TECHNIQUE

Tracy Zboril and Cara Hewett

CHAPTER 7: THE TECHNIQUE

In Part I, we discussed the principles that form the foundation of the Soul Happy technique. While we do want you to see the benefits of practicing this technique, more than anything, we want you to realize the power you have over your own happiness and health. That's why, in Part II, we're going to cover some practical exercises that you can use to guide your healing.

Some of the exercises we mention in this Part of the book are included in the technique we developed, while others are not. We chose to include exercises outside of our technique to give you as many resources as possible to autonomously lead your journey to happiness and good health. We want you to get as much out of this reading as possible, so feel free to use the exercises we've included in a way that works best for you.

Our goal for Part II is for you to walk away feeling more empowered and well-resourced. As the Soul Happy technique is our architype for the new paradigm of self-guided therapy, we will be demonstrating the principles in Part I through the vantage point of this technique. However, we want to make it clear that we believe there are many paths to self-realization and fulfillment. Should you choose to specifically follow the Soul Happy technique, we'd be happy to guide you. Otherwise, we certainly hope you find the practical information included hereafter to be helpful and inspiring.

Since we will be discussing the applications of what you learned in Part I through the lens of the Soul Happy model, let's look at the technique in more detail. The model is delivered through four guided sessions and instructions on how to continue a daily practice. Briefly, here is what the program entails:

Session One - Education

This informational session includes some of the material we have discussed in Part I of this book. It's important that you understand the why's and how's behind the model, so in this session, we succinctly detail the neuroscience that makes the exercises so effective.

Session Two – Clearing the Cluster

In this session, we show you how you can access your subconscious mind. Once there, we demonstrate a selection of active and engaging exercises to clear out the clusters of accumulated negative memories.

Session Three – Expanding Your Awareness

Next is the expanded awareness piece. This is an incredibly moving guided meditation where we go deeper into slowing down the mind. The goal here is to help you to get in touch with your core where your strengths exist in their purest form.

Session Four – Reprogramming Through Sensory Imprinting

Once we've gotten you back in touch with your powerful strengths, you're ready for Imprinting. We once again access the subconscious mind, this time to fill it up with positive, winning scenarios to replace the negativity that's been cleared out.

Ongoing Mental Rehearsal

Lastly, we now need to retrain the conscious mind to be on board with all the transformation that has taken place in the subconscious mind. We do this through short repetition and "mental rehearsal," a widely-used and effective technique that emerged from our study of Dr. Joe Dispenza's valuable work.

Again, there are many paths that lead to the end result – a positive, healthy mind – and the Soul Happy technique is one. In the following chapters, we're going to go over each of the 5 steps listed above. We'll connect each step back to the information we shared in Part I. You'll learn the details of what to expect from each session, the philosophy behind each step, and what reactions and changes to expect along the way.

Our hope is that you can use the information in Part II to build a strong understanding as a solid foundation for a healing experience, but to fully realize the benefit of these techniques, you'll need to experience them first hand. You'll be able to practice some of them by reading our descriptions and instructions, but while we'd love for you to be able to experience sustainable change by reading this book, we can't expect this reading to act as a sufficient substitute for an informed, daily practice. As discussed in Chapter 3, you'll need to be in a certain entranced, brain wave state to really make any long-lasting impact.

Before we dive in, we first want to address a critical component to the work – having an appropriate space and mindset from the start. Because this technique involves deep states of mind and slower brain waves, you'll need to set yourself up for success right from the gate. This means having the appropriate, distraction-free environment to work from, along with a solid understanding of mindfulness and how to achieve it.

Tracy Zboril and Cara Hewett

CHAPTER 8: GETTING SET UP

Before you begin any self-directed practice that focuses on your mind, body, or spirit, it's important to get yourself in the right space, both physically, environmentally and consciously. To really work on yourself, the space you occupy, both inside and outside of yourself, should reflect the state of mind you want to achieve. A messy space or a busy mind can impact your ability to achieve inward peace and outward order.

For the rest of this book, we're going to be talking about some very inward-focused work. This isn't work you can do while driving or even on your lunch break. This is the type of work that takes dedication and intention. It's work that requires self-reflection, and that's not easy to achieve when there's anything else vying for your attention.

Even if you don't plan on following through with the Soul Happy technique, we encourage you to take the guidance offered in this chapter. It can be applied to any other therapeutic model, meditation practice, or simply just quiet, relaxing time for yourself.

Set Up Your Space

Examining your own thoughts and actions is impossible when chaos is all around you. That's why you it's vital to clear a space and make it yours. This space should be exclusively yours (at least for the moment), and it needs to be removed from any tempting or unwanted distractions and interruptions.

We'd like to encourage you to set yourself up in a special area of your own home. Think of this area as your soul space – a space that allows for quiet reflection. Ideally, this "soul space" will give you a private place in your own home to find peace and get the best possible benefit from your journey.

Try to take a few minutes now to think about where in your home you can make a quiet space for yourself. Maybe a little alcove in a bedroom, or a chair in the corner somewhere. Make sure it's somewhere you can sit comfortably and upright. If there's a window nearby and you can see nature, that's great, but not necessary.

Think of a place where it's easy to control the lighting, and where you can add ambiance boosters like a scented candle, which are great for stimulating your sense of smell and offering a zen focal point with the flame. Adding blankets and pillows can round out the coziness, but make sure the space isn't so comfortable that you end up falling asleep.

Set Up Your Time

Setting up your soul space is the easy part. Finding the time to use this space will take some planning. To get the most out of any self-directed therapeutic model, you will need to carve out enough time to complete the introductory steps and then time each day to work on the follow-up exercises. If you're like us, creating time for yourself is not easy. We get it. In today's busy world, it might require planning. Just do it. It's an investment in you. If you need inspiration, think about Cara's client, a grandmother of fourteen kids, all of whom lived with her in a one-bedroom apartment! She found her soul space on her toilet.

Set Up Your Mind

Let's talk about that about that elusive state called "mindfulness." If you've ever come across a mindfulness meditation course, you might be put off by the term. Some online courses and in-person classes encourage you to sit quietly for 30 minutes or more and attempt to become aware of and identify small shifts in the environment like a noise, shape or color. Many people find this excruciating and get turned off by the idea of mindfulness altogether.

This is unfortunate because mindfulness is a valuable state of mind, and it doesn't have to be achieved through boring or tedious exercises. The goal of mindfulness is to appreciate all the beauty, all around you and to slow down your mind. It's the opposite of what most of us do, which is race through our days in a blur moving from one task to the next.

We believe you can achieve the outcome without the excruciating exercise. Every time you get in your car throughout the day, take a few seconds of each drive to simply notice what you're driving past. Let something in nature register in your mind. That's all. If you're on an ugly stretch of highway, take a quick look at the sky and let the pattern of clouds register. That's all. If you see a bird fly by, take notice. That's all.

The more you deliberately do this, the sooner it will become a habit, and the more often you'll find yourself registering fleeting thoughts like, "Wow, those are pretty blooms." Then, five minutes later, "That's cool architecture." And ten minutes later, "Look at that cute kid." You've just been mindful because at its core, mindfulness is simply being in the moment.

The next step you can take toward becoming more mindful is to stop being a multi-tasker. Period. We know it's a source of pride for so many of us, but your multitasking proficiency means that you can respond to any number of situations at once while never fully focusing on any one of them. That means you never fully focus on the people you respond to either - your child, your boss, your spouse, and any other friends and family in your life.

When you look at multitasking from this angle, are you still proud of yourself knowing you've been giving your spouse and children a mere fraction of your attention in any given interaction? Do you think you are enjoying these encounters as much as you could be? After all our efforts to become perfect multitaskers, at the end of the day, we're never fully connected with anything or anyone. Multitasking may make you feel momentarily satisfied with your efficiency, but it will ultimately leave you feeling unfulfilled.

Technology has made our lives eminently more convenient, yet we are more disconnected than ever. We have far less personal interaction with one another because it has been replaced with instant, abbreviated, electronic communication. We all know what it's like to sit in a restaurant and look around the table and notice everyone glancing at their smart phones. There's no judgment here; this has simply become our new normal.

So, you're eating your Caesar salad, glancing at a new text, thinking about your response to that text, half listening to your spouse talk about something that happened that day, and hearing your teen celebrate scoring on the video game on his phone. This is the opposite of mindfulness. You haven't taken the time and care to register the people you love, your surroundings, or even your food. Speaking of food, lack of mindful eating is how so many of us have gained weight over the years.

It's as if we're living in a great social experiment. We celebrate each advancement in technology, yet we are only starting to see some of technology's unintended repercussions.

The Past is Not The Present

In just a moment, we're going to share a simple exercise to help you quickly practice mindfulness. But before we move on, we want to clear up a point of confusion that we see repeatedly in our practice. Bringing this to light will help you become more mindful, because it will help define the present using clearer boundaries.

One of the things that keeps us from living in the present moment is our tendency to ruminate and live in the past. It's a common habit, but one we want to break you of, because the past is nonexistent. It does not exist. To demonstrate this point, let's look at a conversation between Cara and her client, Joe.

Cara: "Joe, does the United States Civil War exist? No really, think about that question, does the Civil War exist?"

Joe: "Well, yes."

Cara: "Does the Civil War exist in the past?"

Joe: "Yes, it did exist."

Cara: "Does the U.S. Civil War exist in the future?

Joe: "Well, no. At least we hope not. "

Cara: "No, the original U.S. Civil War. Does it exist in the future?"

Joe: "Well, no. Not the original one."

Cara: "Is there any way anyone could convince you, Joe, that the original Civil

War exists now or in the future?"

Joe: "Well, no."

Cara: "What about the people who dress up in period costumes and hold muskets in their hands, reenacting the Civil War? Can they convince you that the Civil War exists now or in the future?"

Joe: (laughing) "No, not even them."

This conversation might seem a little on the nose, but it's important to realize that we all tend to play out the past as if it were the present and then project it into the future. When you really focus on the present, you realize that the past and future simply don't exist. They did and they will, but for now, they don't.

Here's another example of one of Tracy's clients, Linda.

Linda has a young adult son who had a rare form of testicular cancer. Her son was successfully treated, and all the scans for the past two years showed no evidence of cancer. Her son went on with his life and was active in college pursuing a career in engineering. Linda, however, was living her life as if her son were still undergoing treatment. Her anxiety levels were off the charts. She woke up every morning assuming the worst. She worried that her son might still have cancer, and that worry completely consumed her thoughts. She was looking for help to move on, to not be obsessed with this constant state of panic.

It might be easy to look at something so far-removed from us, like the Civil War, and place it in the past. But it can be difficult to place an event in the past when it's so deeply attached to our emotions. This was the case for Linda, but despite her emotions, the facts were:

Linda's son did have cancer.
Linda's son was successfully treated for cancer.
Linda's son does not have cancer now.
Linda's son is actively pursuing his own life, cancer free.

Yet Linda was reliving her son's cancer diagnosis and treatment every day to the point of obsession. For Linda, the Civil War was still going on each and every day. She was living the past as if it were the present. Her thoughts, emotions, and behaviors were completely dictated by a past event.

Our rational minds can see that the cancer, Civil War, fill-in the blank trauma doesn't really exist in the present, but our subconscious minds hold the memory and all the attached feelings, making it difficult to let go. When we recall the memory, we recall the feelings and suddenly, what was once in the past is very much in the present. It is the negative (or positive) attachments to any event that cause us to relive them as if they are present moments.

It happens all the time, and quite often we even go so far as to project the past into the future by creating the scenario again and again – worrying and imagining what the future might hold should the scenario reoccur. Even though the logical part of our mind tells us differently, we are hijacked by the emotional intensity of the original trauma.

This unfortunate paradigm is the underlying cause of the psychological labels known as stress, anxiety and depression. By learning to truly be in the present, where the past and future do not exist, we can live our lives without all the angst.

As we've discussed, the subconscious mind is the driving force behind thoughts, feelings, and behavior. Whatever is stored there is pulling the strings. Therefore, the goal is to shift the subconscious mind in a positive direction. Ideally, the best way we know of, is to clear and reboot the subconscious mind so that the understanding of the present becomes the new perspective.

A Mindfulness Exercise

Mindfulness looks great on paper, as a theory, but it's quite a different reality (an even better one) to experience it. While the following is not an exercise we present in the Soul Happy technique, we want to give you a chance to feel what it's like to be mindful.

Once you've got your soul space all set up and ready to go and you've set aside the time, practice the following exercise. It's a great way to quickly get inside the present moment and feel how peaceful and calm it is there. Even taking just three minutes each day to do this little exercise will be amazingly beneficial.

Get yourself in a seated position, preferably in your soul space.

Close your eyes and find your pulse by placing two fingers on the side of your neck. Feel for the rhythmic beat of the strong carotid artery. Spend a few minutes sensing the rhythm. Be in tune with it.

Next, place your two fingers on the underside of the wrist. Just contemplate it. It is fainter. Begin to feel its rhythm. Tune into its beat. Notice how you automatically become calmer.

Next, begin to associate the rhythm with its source, the heart. Visualize the pulsing heart as it beats. Or, if you prefer, you can picture the universal heart symbol. Imagine your heart beating. Sense the love you feel.

Next, place your fingers, or the palm of your hand, over your heart. Even though the sense of rhythm is fainter, contemplate the vibration, the frequency your heart emanates. Start to pay more attention to your heart.

Once the focus is on your heart, imagine your heart becoming in sync with your mind. This coherence is creating a sense of peace. As you contemplate the coherence, visualize the connection you have created.

Next, drop your fingers, still paying close attention to your heartbeat. Sense it; feel it; hear it. Contemplate and just be. Stay with it for a few minutes, then a few minutes more.

CHAPTER 9: STEP 1 - EDUCATION

Session One acts as an overview of how the mind works. Since we've gone over the details of this information in Part I, we want to offer you some additional material that isn't covered in the online version of our technique and a chance to experience the practical applications of that material. The information we are going to detail in this Chapter is not included in the Soul Happy technique. Rather, it includes bonus tools you can use to awaken yourself to the information you read in the previous chapters.

Since so much of the information in Part 1 was a technical review of the subconscious mind, this chapter gives you the chance to become more intimate with your own subconscious and not just experience it from the universal technicalities we presented earlier. By the end of this chapter, you'll be awakened to how your mind has held on to memories, uses those memories as reminders of past traumas, triggers thoughts and feelings, and what you need to do to access the subconscious, which sets the stage for the rest of the exercises in the following chapters.

The Three Factors That Determine Everything

To begin, we want to discuss something with you that we haven't covered yet, and that's atmospheric conditions. Everything in life that happens, happens because of the atmospheric conditions surrounding the event, the genetic coding of the parties involved, and the energy that's directed toward the event. That might be easy to understand on a very analytical level, but let's take a deeper look at what atmospheric conditions really mean.

To understand why anything happens as it does, it's important to see that everything that happens is a direct result of the prior thing that happened, which is a direct result of the thing that happened prior to that. That might sound like a puzzle, but it's the classic pattern of cause and effect. To help you begin to think in this kind of linear, sequential way, we're going to tell you a short story.

In Chapter 5, we discussed the concept that the subconscious mind learns information through story-telling and metaphors. In ancient times, before the written word, stories were used to relay information through generations. The stories that were told always exemplified a theme, a deeper meaning that the storyteller wished to impress upon the listeners. So, let's take a look at a story now that demonstrates the consequent nature of events.

Picture a second-grade teacher and a little boy student. They are the first to arrive on the playground during recess. It's a beautiful spring day; clouds are floating in the sky; children are beginning to pile out of their classrooms, screaming with delight. The student and teacher approach an old, beloved oak tree on the playground and see that a huge branch of the tree is laying on the ground. The little boy says, "Uh oh! How do you think that happened? I love that tree!"

The teacher answers, "Remember that big thunderstorm that came through last night? It must have been the strong wind, or even lightning, that brought that big branch down."

The little boy, distraught, says, "I heard that loud storm too, but why did it have to come here?"

The teacher explains, "Well, that storm is a result of a weather pattern that happened miles away. As it built up momentum, the atmospheric conditions directed it and the weather pattern happened to push it this way, toward our school playground."

The little boy asks, "But why did the weather pattern push the storm toward us?"

"Well, those atmospheric conditions actually started maybe weeks ago off the coast of Cuba, or maybe months ago off the coast of Africa, and the atmospheric conditions were building speed and direction according to the pressures. The storm may have been pushed first in one direction, then in another, then yet another direction, all the while gaining traction and strength. Whichever way it got here, what's important to understand is that it could not have played out any other way than exactly how it did."

The little boy then says, "Okay, I understand that the storm could not have happened any other way. But what about that branch and where it fell. Was that also due to atmospheric conditions?"

"Yes, it was,"

"But then, why did the tree have to be in this exact same spot?"

"Well, that has to do with something completely different--DNA and genetic coding. Over at least 100 years ago, an acorn was carried by the wind or maybe even a bird, and eventually landed right here as the breeze slowed down. Where it landed, and the soil in the ground, had exactly the nutrients that it had. And those nutrients, along with the amount of rainfall, helped the seed germinate, take root, and grow. If the soil had a different makeup of nutrients, or if there had been more rain, the tree may have grown faster or bigger. But the amount of sun, rain, and nutrients it got made the tree grow exactly as it did, and in the exact shape with the branch being

71

exactly where it was. It could not have happened any other way."

"Okay," says the boy. "I understand that it couldn't have grown any other way. It couldn't have been any different than what it was."

Then, the principal of the school walks toward the teacher and the student. She gazes up at the tree and says, "Oh look at that old tree branch; I am so grateful that the branch came down!"

The little boy exclaims, "Why would you be happy about that?"

The principal then explains that she had just been informed by the yard maintenance man that the branch was diseased, and the tree was going to have to come down anyway. It posed a danger to the students on the playground.

The principal says that it was possible the tree could be spared now that the diseased part was gone.

The teacher turns to the student and says, "There's another example of atmospheric conditions. The branch was diseased, weakening its strength, adding to the probability of the wind bringing it down. That's possibly a good thing for the tree and for the students playing around it."

The point of this story is that things happen in our lives in only the exact way they can, due to the atmospheric conditions that have been created throughout our lives, along with our DNA or genetic coding. There is an interconnectivity. Our desires, dreams, and wishes enter the equation in the form of energy - the energy of our thoughts. All three aspects are equally important: atmospheric conditions, genetic coding, and our thoughts.

How Atmospheric Conditions Affect Us

Here's another story to further illustrate how these concepts play out in our lives. This is a true story you might have heard about in the news. It happened in the New York subway a few years back.

> A man was walking along the subway platform and accidently bumped shoulders with another man. The bumped man was so offended that he reacted by shoving the guy with such force that he fell onto the train tracks. A subway train could be heard in the distance. A group of teens was standing nearby. One teen sprang into action, ran toward the tracks, jumped down, grabbed the guy, and with help from the other teens, pulled him up to safety

Let's analyze this from the perspective of atmospheric conditions. It might be easy to perceive a victim, villain, and hero in this story, but try to abstain from judging, and simply look at the situation as a collection of sequential events and circumstances. We're going to be operating on conjecture, not fact, to prove a point, so bear that in mind as you proceed.

Consider why someone might push someone else. What kind of atmospheric conditions and genetic coding might have existed that would result in a person who'd casually push someone into harm's way? Perhaps a lifetime of neglect and/or abuse would lead to thoughts of fear and anger. This man might have lived in a constant state of paranoia, assuming everyone is out to get him. From his potentially warped perspective, he could have interpreted an innocuous bump from a stranger on a subway platform as something far more sinister and intentional.

Also consider that according to the laws of cause and effect, if we had lived the same experiences this man had lived, from the mundane to the monumental moments in his life, and if we had his exact DNA, along with whatever potential chemical imbalances he lived with, we might have responded the same way. Again, this is guesswork, but it stands to reason that it could have been a series of circumstances that led to his choice.

To put this in a relevant contextual framework, imagine the atmospheric conditions that create a whole culture immersed in hatred toward another culture – terrorists. You might not be able to comprehend a society in which children are trained to kill on behalf of patriotism or cultural loyalty, simply to further a mission of death and destruction, but those societies do exist. We must, sadly, acknowledge this takes place.

Now let's look again at our subway teens. Look at the one who jumped on the tracks to lift the man to safety. Imagine the atmospheric conditions that boy grew up with. It's possible he grew up with a solid foundation of love, compassion, and belief in a world of opportunity where anything is possible. His genetic coding could have provided him with a mind that was able to react quickly, and with a willingness to put himself in harm's way to pull a total stranger to safety. If he grew up believing anything was possible, he would automatically embrace the belief that saving this man's life was possible.

What about the teen's friends? They didn't initially react but were still able to assist the teen who jumped onto the tracks. What were their atmospheric conditions? They might not have initially seen any chance of saving the man, but they were ultimately able to respond in a compassionate way. Everyone has different levels of what they think is possible, but their friend's optimism could have swayed them toward his belief system.

What Are Your Atmospheric Conditions?

To further explain the concept of atmospheric conditions, let's examine yours. Take a few moments to consider your culture, your upbringing, and your life experiences.

Was your home strict?
Religious?
Laid-back?
Full of love?
Full of neglect?
Full of fear?
Full of judgement?
Full of shame?

Full of humor?
Full of guilt?
Full of disease?
Full of anger?
Full of security?

What were your atmospheric conditions growing up? How do they relate to your perception of how you, as an adult, view your world? Spend some time considering your atmospheric conditions as an adult. Is your life full of ease and love, or is their anger, hostility, frustration? How is your health? Is your home life disorganized and chaotic? Are you in a quieter phase of your life? Are you wearing many hats?

Take some time to think about your atmospheric conditions, to contemplate how these conditions have shaped who you are. Think about experiences that have caused you to feel disappointment, failure, or trauma. These stored conditions add to the clusters in the subconscious mind.

If you really take this to heart, you can consider your own atmospheric conditions and genetic coding and your own constant thoughts and realize that things have played out in a sequence of cause and effect. In a loving, kinder world, we could begin to stop judging ourselves and others, and appreciate the atmospheric conditions that have brought about everything we experience.

For anyone who has ever wanted to become a better version of themselves, imagine how powerful the concept of a shift in perspective is. It can accomplish all the following:

The perspective of fear becomes one of love.
The perspective of frustration becomes one of calm.
The perspective of anger becomes one of peace.
The perspective of shame becomes one of respect and pride.
The perspective of guilt becomes one of freedom.
The perspective of sadness becomes one of lightness and joy.
The perspective of insecurity becomes one of knowingness.

You can see how powerful this practice can be. Of all the above examples, we believe fear to be the most prevalent and most paralyzing.

The Role of Fear in Your Life

Let's look again at our teen in the subway. It's safe to say that young man who jumped down onto the track was operating fearlessly. His buddies demonstrated various levels of fear, and some might even have been initially paralyzed by the scene. If we go back to our no-judgment concept, the other teens, though well-intentioned, were held back from jumping onto the tracks due to various levels of fear. Wouldn't you rather be the one boy who fearlessly sprang into action? Whether you're facing a job challenge, a new life situation, or a new relationship, wouldn't you rather approach any of these scenarios without fear?

Decreasing fear leads to an increase in performance. Many of our most celebrated humans got where they are today by refusing to let fears hold them back. Steve Jobs and Oprah Winfrey provide two examples. Neither of them gave up on their vision or their mission, no matter how many challenges or setbacks they encountered. They remained tenacious and steadfast. We would say both individuals, when it comes to life aspirations, are fearless. Fearlessness, in this framework, is the goal. When we decrease fear, we are naturally increasing trust in ourselves and our abilities.

We all know what it feels like to walk away from a situation knowing we did not handle ourselves well. Maybe we've been short-tempered with a child, spouse, or colleague. Rather than feeling critical of ourselves, what if we could take a few minutes to think about the atmospheric conditions that led up to the exchange? Sometimes, it's simply a sequence of mundane things such as getting caught in traffic, being insulted by a coworker, feeling overwhelmed with obligations, etc. Rather than getting caught up in judging yourself and your actions, try to understand the factors that led to your behavior and let this awareness help you move forward. It's the new awareness of the situation that provides the shift.

We've hammered this point home about atmospheric conditions because grasping these concepts can truly change your perspective about who you are, where you come from, and how you became the person you are today – all without negative judgement and fear. While this information is outside of the Soul Happy technique, we believe it serves to further your understanding of the subconscious mind and how it operates, which is foundational to the work described in the following chapters.

CHAPTER 10: STEP 2 - CLEARING THE CLUSTER

The Clearing process is where the real power of this technique begins. In this step, you'll be able to put all the knowledge you've learned thus far into very practical and tangible steps. Once you gain conscious access to the subconscious mind, you'll work with self-directed tools that powerfully clear out the memories of failure, disappointment, embarrassment, and further negative emotions that interfere with you being able to be the best version of yourself.

This process is exciting, and the effects are felt quickly, but like anything worthwhile, it does take time and effort. Aim to commit yourself to taking as much time as needed. All the knowledge you've accumulated thus far gives you an advantage. Understanding, even at a very basic level, the science behind the exercises adds power to what are already very potent tools.

The tools in this step are designed to clear away the accumulated negative emotions by scrambling how the brain routes the information through the synapses and neural pathways. This transmutes the original vibrational energy of emotion into a new vibrational energy.

When you recount a memory, electrical currents run through neural pathways. If you interrupt the retelling of the memory, the electrical currents stop and instead head down a new neural pathway, forming a new synapse. With every interruption, the electricity continues down new neural pathways. This is how the scrambling transpires and the emotion attached to the memory becomes diluted.

Once this scrambling and subsequent dilution has taken place, you won't have to filter through the accumulated debris as you react to a stressful situation. Your mind will be cleared, opening space for wise, grounded reactions. The memory doesn't go away; it simply stops carrying intense feelings. Intense feelings attached to memories cloud reality. By clearing them, you free yourself from their interference.

Recalling Traumas

The first step to clearing intense feelings attached to memories, whether you're conscious of them or not, is to find the trauma they are attached to. Trauma sounds intimidating, but in this context, it's referring to any situation that's affecting your day to day life.

Traumas can be related to your career, personal life, or any situation that you suspect has affected your view of yourself or your self-confidence. We encourage anyone going through the exercise not to get too caught up in picking the memory. Instead, we suggest you chose one that generally depicts a disappointment or a failure. You can trust that your subconscious mind knows how to include other memories that have had a similar emotional impact.

Examples of business trauma could be as extreme as being fired from a job, or as small as dealing with a disgruntled client. An example of a personal trauma might be a failed relationship, poor parenting choices, having a hard time controlling your anger, or having experienced an abusive or violent incident. Again, it isn't necessary to get too caught up in which memories to choose, and there's no need to pick "the worst thing that's ever happened." This process works by targeting emotions, and emotions tend to be attached to many traumas. Picking any trauma will target the cluster of attached memories and emotions.

In the Soul Happy technique, we ask you to choose 3 traumas – one from adulthood, early adulthood or teenage years, and then one from childhood. For example, you might choose the memories attached to a recent professional rejection, then a bad breakup from your early 20s, and then a time when someone humiliated you as a child. Or, you might choose a misstep in parenting from a few years back, a time when you were rejected in high school, and then a scary injury from childhood.

It's your choice how intense you want to go with these memories. It's likely that the most intense and profound moments of your life are taking up a lot of space through smaller attached memories. If you'll recall from Chapter 3, one intense experience can be reexperienced repeatedly, and each time a situation reminds you of the initial experience, the cluster of that memory will grow. In this way, it's not critical that you choose an intense trauma like abuse or a death. You certainly can, but just be aware that going right to the source of the cluster can cause a disassociation or become too intense too quickly before you're able to scramble the memory. If that occurs, choose a less intense experience. You'll likely still be working with the same cluster.

At this point, there are several techniques you can use to scramble the associated emotions. Whatever method you choose, it's important to bring your mind into the brain wave state we talked about in Part I. In the Soul Happy technique, we guide you to this state through breathing exercises and suggestions. It's only in this relaxed, yet conscious state, that clearing can begin to take place.

Scrambling the Emotional Intensity

To scramble the emotional intensity associated with a memory, you'll need to recall the memory in as much vivid detail as possible. Because senses are the language of the subconscious, we encourage you to recall as many senses from the memory as possible. What can you taste, feel, smell, hear, and see specifically?

We've mentioned before that when you're reading this book, you're in a very active brainwave state called beta. In this state, it might seem difficult to recall memories so vividly, especially if you're working with a childhood memory. But remember, once you're in a more relaxed state, you'll be on the threshold of your subconscious and the vivid memories will easily be able to come forward.

Once the memory has been recalled, we encourage you to experience its vibrational energy. This is an important step because it helps you practice seeing things as they are. If you recall the information from Chapter 5, you'll remember that everything is energy – even these experiences that might seem very real during their recollection. They do not exist in the present. They are energy. Bring your awareness to their distinct energy signature.

Then the clearing happens. This is a very experiential part of the process and if you choose to attempt our technique, we will guide you through a series of physical movements and postures designed to confuse the synapses firing in your brain. Where your mind will want to fully envelop you in the memory, you'll be confusing it with active motions that activate other parts of your brain not associated with the memory. This serves to break up the intensity of the emotion.

The concept behind this process is to allow you to experience the memory without reliving it. There are many very effective ways to achieve this, including the well-known tapping motions of the Emotional Freedom Technique. We suggest experimenting with the techniques that feel right for you. The goal is to simultaneously recall an intense memory and show your mind that you are still in the present. Once you've achieved this, the vibrational energy of the memory will quickly start to shift.

- The vibrational energy of rage shifts to a vibrational energy of peace.
- The vibrational energy of guilt shifts to one of freedom.
- The vibrational energy of insecurity shifts to the vibrational energy of knowingness.
- The vibrational energy of shame shifts to the vibrational energy of pride.
- The vibrational energy of frustration shifts to the vibrational energy of calmness.
- The vibrational energy of sadness shifts to the vibrational energy of happiness.
- The vibrational energy of fear shifts to the vibrational energy of love.

During this process, your subconscious will naturally scan back and attach the new energetic shift to any relatable memories. All memories with a similar energetic signature are attached, and your mind will instantly connect the new experience to those memories.

Once the first memory has been reassigned a new energy, you can repeat the exercise with the memory from early adulthood and then childhood. Each time, you'll need to get in the right brainwave state, recall the memory with as much sensory detail as possible, and then scramble the connections using your chosen technique.

Outside of EFT, other effective tools to scramble memories are humor and shifting perspectives. In other words, you can use humor or surprise to detach the negative intensity of the emotion from its well-worn path or you can use certain suggestions to view your memory from a greater distance or height. In our technique, we employ two scrambling activities for each of the three memories.

The Final Sweep

Once you've gone through the exercises to redirect the emotional intensity of the memories, it can be helpful to run through a final clearing sweep to make sure the redirection was successful. If there are any stragglers, you can use a visualization exercise to clear those leftover blocks. This isn't an exercise we include in our technique, but we do believe it is very helpful and effective, so we've included it here as a bonus.

To do the exercise, try to think of people in your life that you have negative feelings towards. Attempt to land on three individuals that trigger you. Singling one of them out, think about all the things that person has done that have rubbed you the wrong way.

This exercise isn't meant to be invalidating in any way. Negative emotions are important in the moment. They guide us to realizations about ourselves and our boundaries. But, eventually, those feelings no longer serve a purpose. Once you've learned what you needed to know from an experience, the feeling clogs up the system and keeps you from moving on.

In the end, harboring negativity about someone only serves to harm you. If you've already reacted appropriately to the situation, whether its removing that person from your life or changing your expectations and boundaries, then the negativity has already done its job.

It's at this point that you can use the information you learned about atmospheric conditions. Consider what you know about that individual and what the roots of that behavior might be. More often than not, we've found that unhealthy behaviors are rooted in insecurity, and you'll probably find this to be true when you examine the atmospheric conditions of the person you're considering.

Why did Hitler need to come up with the perfect race?
Why did Osama Bin Laden train young men to kill?
Why does your co-worker throw you under the bus?
Why is your mother-in-law so critical of you?

When you recall these emotions, you'll more than likely realize that this person's reaction to their insecurity has triggered a reaction in you based on your insecurities. This cycle is called mirroring, or shadowing, as introduced by Carl Jung and made popular by many self–help authors including Debbie Ford.

In the mirroring theory, your negative qualities can be identified in any person you are judging – what you are uncomfortable with about yourself is mirrored back as judgement against another. Logically, that might make sense, but it can be quite a leap to see it in yourself, so, in this model, we are not asking you to try to identify these shared qualities. We've found that it is enough for you to acknowledge that you and this person share the universal trait of insecurity.

This does not mean, however, that you both react in the same ways when your insecurity is triggered. You might have opposite reactions. But if you feel you have nothing in common with this person, and cannot relate to them in any way, you can be certain that you both share insecurity.

Just as in the first exercise, this process is most effective when you recall memories of a person with as much sensory detail as possible. Doing so will trigger the root of the emotional intensity and allow you to access the real memory and clear it. Once you've done this, consider the atmospheric conditions of insecurity that are the common denominator between you and this person. As you do so, the emotional intensity around the person and the memory will begin to lift.

You can repeat this exercise with as many people as you like, but we've found that three times is very effective. In the end, you will have replaced the negative feelings and judgement with compassion and empathy. This won't mean that any work you've done with boundaries or expectations will change. Rather, it means that the negative feelings, which no longer serve a purpose, will now be replaced with healthy, useful emotions.

It's a good idea to take a moment to observe and reflect on the changes that occur after the exercise is complete. Whether you simply ponder it for a few moments or jot some notes down in a journal, changes are always more solidified through conscious observation. Observation is also powerful because it lets you really enjoy your hard work and experience how easily energy can shift.

CHAPTER 11: STEP 3 - EXPANDING YOUR AWARENESS

Clearing away clusters of intense emotions attached to trauma frees up access to your core self. Think of it like a traffic jam. An accident causes stop and go traffic and angry, impatient drivers react poorly causing more accidents and traffic slows down even more. This is just like the negative clusters in your subconscious – a traumatic event causes an intense emotion and then more and more negative reactions pile up creating an even bigger cluster. But just like how an interstate full of patient, level-headed drivers allows everyone to get to their destination safely and on time, clearing away the clusters in your mind creates space to freely navigate to your destination, in this case, your core self.

In Dr. Wayne Dyer's book, *Living an Inspired Life*, Dr. Dyer beautifully describes why we need to connect with the core of who we are. Dr. Dyer writes, "The feelings of emptiness, the idea that there must be something more; wondering 'Is this all there is?' and trying to determine the meaning of life . . . this is all evidence of a yearning to connect with our soul. We are aching for our calling to be felt and expressed."

Connecting with your core self is a profound and beautiful experience. That connection isn't something that can be experienced through reading a book, so you'll need to take part in some form of meditation or exercise to achieve it. In this chapter, we are going to discuss the exercises we use to help clients become reacquainted with their strengths in their purest form.

Again, there are many tools you can use to make this connection, but we've found the that techniques described are very effective at opening the lines of communication between a soul and its host. When you open that line of communication, you'll find that your desires become clear and you start to become the best possible version of yourself. Your core holds all the answers to everything you'd ever need to know about who you are and why you're here.

Listen to Your Soul

To discover those answers, not only do you have to meet your soul, you have to be able to listen to it. When you first attempt to listen, you'll quickly learn what your conscious mind sounds like and what its function is. The voice of the conscious mind isn't always in contrast to the core voice, but it is much louder. Many times, the conscious voice is coming from a place of caution or fear. Its purpose is to protect and survive, and it is very, very loud and clear with those messages.

How can you quiet down the voice of the conscious mind so that you're able to hear your core voice? The key is learning to distinguish between the messages. The conscious voice might be loud and repetitive, but your core voice is still present. Tuning in, finding the voice and developing a relationship with your core self will help you learn how to listen more closely.

While we're clearly passionate about everything in this book, our most significant drive is teaching people how to look inward for answers. So if you take away one point from everything you've read, we hope that it's the knowledge that all the answers lie within you. We want to empower you to turn inward. The technique we developed is merely a tool to help you reach this realization and act on it. Strengthening the habit of looking inward helps everyone decrease their need for outward guidance, acceptance and acknowledgement. That is the power of listening to the inner voice.

In the book *How to Get What You Really, Really, Really Want*, co-authored by Dr. Wayne Dyer and Dr. Deepak Chopra, the authors state that the best way to manifest (attract) what you want into your life is to "banish all doubt" from your mind and "know" that you can get it. They contend that we must seek independence from concern over others' opinions.

All of us, since childhood, have been indoctrinated by society, governments, culture and for some, organized religion, that have bound us with dogmas, regulations, laws, beliefs, and rules. As a result, we look to outward governing bodies to direct us. We rely on external sources, and when we do so, we neglect to develop independent, original thinking.

Instead of being encouraged to have an inward focus for guidance, it has become the norm to look outward. We often seek approval from everyone but ourselves. This habit goes away without a fight when you begin to inquire within. The success you achieve on your inner work and the stronger you build your connection to you core self, the less you rely on others for validation.

Realize Your Optimal Potential

The emphasis on external information and stimulus is everywhere, but as you begin to practice the art of inquiring within, the habit dies. Of course, it is easier said than done, at first, but once you get a taste of the confidence and empowerment that comes from your core self, you'll never look back. Once you get comfortable touching in with your center and your core, it will become a space you will yearn for.

You will come to deeply realize who you are at your core, where all your strengths exist in their purest form, before you fell victim to life's disappointments, failures, and your attempts to fit into society with all its damaging messages. When we've brought clients to this state, they've described feelings like a sense of pure peace, calm, love, and knowingness. It is a powerful place to reach because it means you've gotten in touch with who you really are, your authentic self.

This is your inner voice, deep down, that wants to guide you, and it will only guide you for good. The only thing interfering with its ability to help you is the fact that over the years, you've stopped listening. Within this quiet knowingness, all possibilities exist. Who wouldn't want to live there?

In the Soul Happy model, we guide our clients through a powerful meditation that can generate significant results. There are many guided meditations out there, but it can be tricky to find an effective, high-quality one. We developed our meditation within the context of our model to immediately follow the clearing session. You'll know a guided meditation to engage with your core self is working when you experience the calm, confident feelings described at the beginning of this section.

Whatever tool you use to engage with your core self, you'll be left feeling aligned with your strengths and you'll be more likely to consistently respond to life in ways that make you proud – your optimal potential. Ultimately, we envision that any guided imagery or meditation can be utilized often. The more time you spend in this optimal state, which represents the best version of you, the better your life will be. This is the goal of our development of this model.

Why Inquire Within?

In Ralph Waldo Emerson's classic essay, *The Over-Soul,* he writes, "The soul is the perceiver and revealer of truth. We know truth when we see it, let skeptic and scoffer say what they choose. Foolish people ask you, when you have spoken what they do not wish to hear, 'How do you know it is truth, and not an error of your own?' We know truth when we see it, from opinion, as we know when we are awake that we are awake. It was a grand sentence of Emanuel Swedenborg, which would alone indicate the greatness of that man's perception,--'It is no proof of a man's understanding to be able to confirm whatever he pleases; but to be able to discern that what is true is true, and that what is false is false,--this is the mark and character of intelligence.'"

The point we're making here is that when you confidently begin looking inward for guidance, you can train yourself to recognize a knowingness that sets you apart from others. The more comfortable you get listening to your intuitive voice, which some call your higher self, the more it will become your truth. When this occurs, your intelligent and authentic self will prevail.

Mr. Emerson's term, "The Over-Soul," is a phrase referred to in mystical and philosophical writings. This concept of the Over-Soul is often referred to by leaders in the fields of psychology as the Super Conscious. Carl Jung also refers to the Super Conscious as the "Collective Unconscious." Our Super Conscious part of us exists at a level where many aspects of consciousness are focused. This brings us to our earlier description of getting you in touch with who you are at your core. Remember, this is where all your strengths exist in their purest form - within the Super Conscious.

As you become more and more familiar residing within your Super Conscious, your inner voice, or your own intuition, will start to become a larger part of who you are. In the more refined realms of the Super Conscious, you can better clarify more inspired direction. Learning to be in touch with your inner voice will be a huge tool for guidance. Your Super Conscious only wants what is best for you.

Isn't it great to know that for the rest of your life, you have (and have always had) your own inner wise one, patiently waiting for you to ask for greater wisdom? Let's make a habit of getting in touch with this wise one more often so we can start making consistently good choices.

Being in touch with the wisest version of yourself is the key to the peace and knowingness we have referred to throughout this book. This is why we love Session Three so much. Our intuition guides our creativity. It is the place where our talents surface. It is said that Einstein existed in this realm, so beware - using this model could lead to brilliance.

Expanded Awareness Meditation

You're probably eager to get in touch with your Super Conscious now. It's a really exciting prospect, and it's the perfect destination after the traffic jam of your clusters has been cleared. In our model, we take you through a deep, guided meditation that brings you to an even calmer brain wave state. You don't need to enter a sleep state to meet your core self, but the less active your conscious mind is, the better your experience will be.

We aim to accomplish this by guiding our clients first through a body relaxation exercise. This is a common technique found at the beginning of many hypnosis and self-hypnosis sessions. In this type of relaxation exercise, you actively work through all your muscle groups to release tension and create a powerful melting sensation. This full body release allows your mind the chance to open further to your subconscious, giving you access to the deepest parts of yourself.

In this very relaxed state, you will be able to meet and connect with your core self, your own inner guidance system. In our technique, we guide you through a visualization that gives you the chance to experience your core self, your soul. You'll feel the sensation of what it's like to be in full knowing of yourself, and you'll get the chance to visualize this special and important part of you.

This experience is often very profound for our clients. Getting in touch with your truest self is an overwhelmingly peaceful experience. There is no greater comfort than coming to know the part of you that has only the best of intentions. Once you've met your true self, it's time to put that inner guidance system to use and prepare your mind for the future.

CHAPTER 12: STEP 4 - REPROGRAMMING THROUGH SENSORY IMPRINTING

Once you've cleared out the clusters and then experienced meeting and connecting with your core self, it's time to do some reprogramming. Going back to our traffic metaphor, you can think of this step as improving the roadways to reduce future accidents. Perhaps new routes need to be developed or dangerous intersections need more safety features. In this step, you'll work with your subconscious to plan out your future routes and make it easier for your core self to be heard. Unlike the traffic scenario, this step is quick, easy, and fun. In our model, we call this process Imprinting because you'll be imprinting positive thoughts and emotions into the newly cleared space.

We've mentioned a few times throughout this book that the language of the subconscious mind is the senses. If we only use words to speak to the subconscious, such as positive affirmations, the subconscious won't be able to fully embrace the true intention. If we use the senses, on the other hand, or feeling, we're speaking the language of the subconscious and it's able to fully digest our intentions and meanings.

To further explain, when someone asks you what you had for dinner last night, you then access the memory bank in your subconscious mind. You immediately access a visual of your meal. If it was particularly memorable, you might even smell or taste it. Let's say it was a salmon Caesar salad. Language does not dictate to you that you had romaine lettuce, parmesan cheese, grilled pink fish, etc. Instead, you experience the sensations of the meal, whether it be what it looked like, smelled like, or tasted like, in your mind's eye.

Using the Language of the Subconscious

When you want to program anything into your subconscious mind, attaching sensory information will enhance the programming and make the message more effective. In other words, instead of relying on merely positive affirmations, if you add images, smells and sounds to the positive affirmation, the programming of that affirmation will bypass your conscious mind and get programmed directly in to your subconscious.

To that end, we employ a visual, audio, smell, and touch element in our model. The visual component is a universal symbol that represents consciousness and a connection to all that is. This symbol becomes the anchor to which you can attach all the other sensory information. When you recall a memory, your first experience is visual. You see the experience in your mind's eye. If it helps, you can think of the subconscious as a series of doors. When the first door is open, you can see an image in your mind's eye. The further you go, the more intense and real the sensations become. This is why, in our model, we use the universal symbol as a foundation to attach the rest of the sensory information.

The next sense we employ is sound. We do this with the mantra, "I am my highest potential." . A mantra is a personal statement often used in a repetitive manner to aid in the concentration of an intended state of being. If you have been in a yoga or meditation class, you understand the importance of repeating the word "om." Om is a Sanskrit word, which in its most simple of terms, represents the universe. The purpose of reciting "om" is to align with the universe. It's a single sound meant to validate oneness and harmony. It is even among the sounds recorded in deep space, according to NASA. In keeping with the theory behind "om," we wanted to come up with a simple, short mantra with a significant, transformational effect.

The next sense we utilize is the sense of scent. We'd like you to explore essential oils and find a scent that is pleasing to you - something that resonates deeply with you when you first experience it. Our recommendation is to choose only one scent. We find that one solitary scent holds more power than combining two or more.

Most health food stores are a great resource for oils because you're able to use a tester to try out the smell before making a purchase. If you're not near a store that sells essential oils, you can try an online retailer like Doterra or Young Living. You won't have the opportunity to test the oils if you order online, but you can follow your instincts and select an oil based on your prior experience with scents like peppermint, lemon, clove, cinnamon, lavender, etc.

The last sense utilized in our model is the kinesthetic sense. Touch is very powerful, especially when employed on a meridian point of the body like the eyebrow or wrist. Using a finger to apply slight pressure can focus energy onto that specific meridian or channel. There are several meridian points, but we have found these two to be the most easily accessible for our clients. Let's say you are going into a high-pressured business meeting and just before you sit down you need a quick dose of self-confidence. You could discreetly apply pressure to either your eyebrow or the inside of your wrist and become grounded, bringing forth feelings of confidence and calm.

The same theory also applies in active situations, like on the tennis court. Putting pressure on the eyebrow is quick and unnoticeable to your opponent. But it alerts the subconscious mind, reminding it of whatever you've programmed it to do. In our model, we show you how to incorporate the kinesthetic method into all the others we've been discussing.

Remember the Future

Once all your sensory information has been chosen and implemented, it's time to put them to use in reprogramming your subconscious mind for the future. Before your clusters are cleared, you operate by unconsciously reacting to situations based on what those clusters have programmed you to do. Once the clusters are cleared, you can program your future reactions to be guided by your core self. This is really where the entire process is tied together.

This part of the process is very specific to our model, so we're going to describe the details of our technique below. As with every step, there are many paths to achieving the goal. In this case, there are many ways to reprogram your subconscious with sensory imprinting. What we are going to describe is the path we guide our clients down. Should you choose the Soul Happy technique, you'll also follow these exact steps.

In our model, we ask you to come up with six future scenarios of success. These scenarios can be business or personal related; it doesn't matter. They should be general, and not too specific. Cast a wide net. Some examples include successfully signing on a new client;

successfully negotiating a new deal; receiving an excellent review; exceeding your sales quota at work; making improvements in an existing relationship; meeting the love of your life; getting a new degree; handling a parenting situation beautifully and effectively; or simply finding balance in your life.

It takes time to come up with the six scenarios, and that's ok, because we're going to ask you to create a visual of them with as much detail as possible. We want you to place yourself directly into the scene as if it were the present moment. You'll imagine yourself looking around and seeing, smelling, hearing, and fully sensing the experience.

We'll also ask you not to just sense the scene, but to feel the scene. You'll expand your positive feelings about the scenario as big as they can go. The subconscious responds to intense emotions (remember Chapter 4?), so the bigger you can feel, the louder it will be to your subconscious.

Unfortunately, negativity gets imprinted just as easily as positivity. You might recall that negative experiences even tend to be stored upfront in our memory banks more predominantly than positive ones. Therefore, it is imperative that you program only bliss and success during this process. You have already cleared the debris, leaving room for these new imprints. Don't inadvertently create more clusters with more negative-thought debris.

After you've fully imagined and felt the scenario, we guide you through the five senses to imprint the feelings. You'll get into a relaxed brain wave state and perform exercises that engage each sense individually. As you do so, you'll be asked to recall the visualization again and then connect it the sensory experiences we described in the previous section.

You'll repeat this exercise with all 6 scenarios that you chose. It is a time-consuming process, but once you've completed it, you will have reprogrammed your subconscious to connect with your truest and wisest self. This programming will be imprinted on your subconscious through the five senses, and we'll teach you how to recall it instantly whenever you need it.

In fact, recalling it frequently is the key to success. Using these tools over and over will train the conscious mind to be on board with the programming that took place in the subconscious mind. This is known as "mental rehearsal," and we'll tell you more about it in the next chapter.

Tracy Zboril and Cara Hewett

92

CHAPTER 13: ONGOING MENTAL REHEARSAL

You've now been taken all the way through the journey of physically changing your mind to stop relying on unconscious, automatic practices, and to instead rely on the voice of your core self. From the research that serves as the foundation, to the four sessions that make the technique so powerful, you've learned a lot. We hope this book has been healing for you in some capacity, and we hope that by the end of this chapter, you will walk away empowered and inspired to literally change your brain and seek the answers from within.

Tools for Rehearsal

Before we say goodbye, we want to cover one more important topic – mental rehearsal. The changes you make in your brain are meant to be sustainable and long-lasting, and to ensure your results stick with you, we encourage you to continue a short, daily practice.

Remember, neural pathways can be strengthened through repetition, and a strong neural pathway means a more automatic reaction. Since you haven't built a habit around this technique yet, we encourage you to invest in some habit-forming aids. Whether you simply set daily reminders on your phone or go so far as to post little notes around your home and office, just make sure that you build a habit around the exercises you've learned. In our model, we include a smart phone app that helps you build these habits in five seconds or less through the use of texting services and daily reminders.

Habits are important because even though relief is experienced as a result of the clearing and imprinting in your subconscious mind, the conscious mind, we have found, needs to be retrained as well. Without this step you're more likely to fall back into old patterns of behavior.

Rehearsal is key.

There are other ways of ensuring repetition, too. To make use of mental rehearsal, you can commit to taking a few minutes every day to reinforce the new paradigm. You can do this anywhere - driving, waiting in line at the grocery store, etc. We encourage you to get creative.

One technique our clients have found helpful is to use your thumb to put pressure on each finger of your hand, one by one, while visualizing the universal symbol, stating your mantra, and smelling the essential oil you chose. The more often you can do it, the better. There's no upper limit to how frequently you can employ this quick reminder technique.

If you do this for at least three months, you will have trained your mind to form a new habit. After three months, continue as much as possible. Make this an ongoing maintenance habit for your mental health. You probably already accept that you need to work out to keep your physical body strong. Think of this as a workout for your mind. Like anything else, it must be practiced.

One way we have found that helps to keep focus on this repetition sequence is to use a mala bead bracelet. An internet search for "mala beads" will show you the kind of bracelet we are referring to. You might even have something in your jewelry box already that resembles a mala bead bracelet. Any beaded bracelet will do. The idea is to touch each bead sequentially while visualizing the symbol and stating the mantra. Go all the way around the bracelet as many times as you like.

Of course, these are just suggestions and creative ways our clients have found to build habits. In the end, you can use whatever method you like to build these habits and increase repetition. Make it a fun and relaxing moment in your day – a brief moment that is all about you.

Final Thoughts

Our deepest gratitude goes out to you and we hope that you will soon begin the journey toward a positive, more fulfilled life by tapping into the deepest roots of your negativity, cutting away the debris, and programming your mind to be the happy, wise, peaceful person you were born to be. In the next section, we've included resources that we hope will guide you on this path. Many of these resources are techniques you can implement on your own without a therapist, like the Emotional Freedom Technique. To learn more about our specific technique, visit http://www.soulhappy.com

RESOURCE LIST

Eye Movement Desensitization and Reprocessing –
http://www.emdr.com/what-is-emdr/

Neurolinguistic Programming - http://www.nlp.com/what-is-nlp/

Emotional Freedom Technique - https://eft.mercola.com/

Deepak Chopra - https://www.deepakchopra.com/

Joe Dispenza - http://www.drjoedispenza.com/

Lynne McTaggert - https://lynnemctaggart.com/

John Kehoe - https://www.learnmindpower.com/

Iyanla Vanzant - https://iyanla.co/

Wayne Dryer - https://www.greggbraden.com/

Bruce Lipton - https://www.brucelipton.com/

Louise Hay - https://www.louisehay.com/

Ekhart Tolle - https://www.eckharttolle.com/